MORTALITY
REALITY

*Why in the World
Did We All Shout for Joy?*

by
Linda R. Archibald

MORTALITY REALITY

Distributed by

Granite Publishing and Distribution, L.L.C.
868 North 1430 West • Orem, UT 84057
(801) 229-9023 • Toll Free (800) 574-5779
FAX (801) 229-1924

Production by www.SunriseBooks.com

ISBN: 1-932280-07-3
Library of Congress Control Number: 2003103244

*This book is dedicated to all those poor souls who, like me,
have been driven to perfection*

CONTENTS

ACKNOWLEDGMENTS

So many have helped me in my personal journey: parents, relatives, friends, teachers—even people in history and protagonists in theater. With specific reference to this work, I express my gratitude—

— to Jeff Lambson at Granite Publishing and to Brian Carter at SunriseBooks.com for their professional support and assistance.

— to gospel teachers who taught me to look deep into the scriptures for answers.

— to Ayrton Senna and his countrymen for initiating my change of heart and my search for understanding.

— to Dallas for constant encouragement: seen and unseen, heard and unheard.

— to Teresa for reminding me daily of the importance of individuality, flexibility, and all the other realities of mortality.

— to Barbara Marchant and the Relief Society sisters in Cedar City for first giving me the opportunity to tell my story—and to Nancy Rappleye and the Relief Society sisters in Nashville for providing a laboratory for me to reformat the material.

— to Jeanne Hatch, Jane Kennedy, Jean Alder, Marilyn Anderson, Gail Rushforth, Anna-Marie Davis, Barbara Dennis, Bonni Jones, Elisa Brough, Carol Jackson, Bill Nixon, Toni Simmons, and LuAnn and Jerry Day—as well as any other friends and acquaintances I may have neglected to mention—who, at various times, kindly listened to my thoughts, read my work, and gave me counsel and correction.

— And a special note of appreciation to Kirk Jones (and to Stacy for allowing me to intrude on their time together) who, over many months, read countless versions of the manuscript and provided valuable feed-back. As I seek various ways to share the lessons I have learned with others, his advice continues to light the way.

HAPPY THOUGHTS?

*Where wast thou when I laid the foundations of the earth?
declare, if thou hast understanding...*

*Whereupon are the foundations thereof fastened? or who
laid the corner stone thereof;*

*When the morning stars sang together, and all the sons of
God shouted for joy?*

(Job 38:4,6,7).

I didn't know how to shout for joy in the present moment. Why in
the world would I have done so then?

I was such an orderly person. "Neat and tidy" was my motto. "A
place for everything and everything in its place." I should have had
some such tribute to organization engraven over my front door—or at

1

least on the broom closet. But although I thought I was trying to follow the scriptural instructions to set my house in order and to press forward steadfastly and endure to the end, this orderliness and effort did not lay a foundation for peace. Instead, it was a catalyst for frustration and discouragement because, in spite of all I could do, I could not make people orderly, I could not make life orderly, and I was imperfect with flaws abounding—something I knew all too well, although I tried not to show it too often.

In short, I was a perfectionist. I wanted precision at all costs; but, no matter how hard I tried, I could not make such perfection happen. As a result of this sense of powerlessness, I created a state of self-made adversity, of resentment, because I was unwilling to accept that those same scriptures which speak so often of order and effort speak just as often of joy:

"Men are, that they might have joy" (2 Nephi 2:25).

"A merry heart doeth good like a medicine" (Prov.17:22).

"Let us be glad and rejoice" (Rev. 19:7).

How could it be possible, I wondered, to follow the instructions to "press forward steadfastly and endure to the end" (doctrines of

2

weariness) and still be glad and rejoice? How could I focus on "be ye therefore perfect" (doctrine of exhaustion) and at the same time have a merry heart? Life was so filled with challenge, with stress, and with never being able to get "all my ducks lined up in a row," that I had no idea where to find any good cheer.

Though the scriptural instruction seemed to be "endure to the end joyfully," I was sure that endurance and joy were incompatible. Nevertheless, I didn't plan to take the rejoice verses out of my scriptures. Rather, I annotated them with "later" or "at another time."

I never doubted my ability to achieve desired eternal rewards. I never thought of giving up the good fight. I never believed I wasn't good enough or capable enough to become all I could be. I just believed that by doing everything required of me, there was no time left for joy. Joy, I thought, would only be found somewhere in the distant future—in another time and place. Joy could never be real today, especially on really bad days.

That's what I believed until the Spirit insisted that I do a reality check. Life events caused me to re-evaluate my perspective on joy and then directed me in a search for scriptural understanding. One scripture, in particular, initiated a major paradigm shift. Father Adam, whose life was hardly a bowl of cherries, spoke to me across time:

"...In this life I shall have joy" (Moses 5:10). In *this* life! *This life!* I compared my idea of "Joy Sometime" to Adam's declaration of "Joy Now" and realized that he must have known the truth.

"But," I questioned, "if 'Joy Now' is true doctrine, why had it eluded me for so long?" The answer, sadly, was that in spite of scripture study, seminary and institute classes, extensive leadership and teaching responsibilities in all church auxiliaries including Sunday School gospel doctrine—and even though I knew the gospel was true—I did not know the gospel. I did not understand mortality's realities. I had allowed unrealistic social expectations to intertwine themselves with gospel principles; and, as a result, I had made the gospel a vehicle for weariness instead of a generator of joy. But when Adam spoke to me from the past about "Joy Now," he jerked me out of my weary, pessimistic mind-set enough that I could stand back and look objectively at possibilities. I went in search of scriptural validation and gospel verification of the proposition "Joy Now," and I found the truth: *There really is a Great Plan of Happiness!*

I learned to sing *"Hallelujah!"*—as I will explain in the following pages. If I could, I would teach the world how to sing it, too.

Picture Perfect
Quicksand

"I thought that if I was just obedient, life would then be easy,
and I could get 'all my ducks lined up in a row,'"—
she mused wistfully, now knowing better.

I was once a lover of precision, reveling in lists efficiently checked
off, neat and tidy drawers and closets, everyone working quietly on
orderly tasks. I adored agendas and to-do lists. I savored a plan well-
made and a plan completed. I valued compliant people. I treasured the
heady idea of perfection and delighted in the sense of order and accomplishment I attempted to create—and on very rare occasions actually
did bring to pass.

Nevertheless, in spite of some success, this orderliness allowed only temporary moments of satisfaction, certainly no hint of permanent joy, because 1) the order never lasted very long and 2) it was never enough. That's the way it is when one is "driven to perfection." Even in success, there is always a sense of failure and distress.

To look at my life on the surface during those days, however, no one would have guessed that I was dealing with discouragement. I appeared to be happy and successful, involved in what should have been an exciting life with a wonderful husband and a beautiful daughter. Beneath the façade, however, was gloom. I was perpetually unhappy and had no idea how I could change, or even if I should change. Taking my cues from society, I thought uniformity was better than individuality and exhaustion was better than exuberance.

I didn't know my perspective was like quicksand. How could I? I was just trying to live the way the "experts"—the motivational, time management, parenting, self-esteem experts—told me to live, trying to value the order, precision, and achievement my society valued. I was so blinded by the propaganda that, even after I fell into the muck, I couldn't see other options. As a result, I kicked at the pressure and screamed at the impossibility of it all. I tried to keep from being sucked under, tried to keep breathing—though once in a while I just stopped fighting and allowed myself to sink. But then my will to survive socially would win and I would fight my way back to the surface where I was required, once again, to face the power of the quicksand, the forces of stress: conform, compete, and achieve—all with inherent, unrealistic expectations.

Being driven to perfection is like that, like being stuck in quicksand.

Perfection, in this modern era, is a companion of competition—a game of who has the *most* and who has the *best*. When we play the game, jump into the quicksand, it is usually because everyone around us seems to be doing it and joining them in the quagmire appears to be the appropriate thing for us to do. Even as the pressure of the quicksand seeks to suck the life out of us, we accept the stress as normal. After all, exhaustion is a lively topic of conversation, ironically, and it garners great social accolades.

As a participant in the game, sometimes I jumped into academic quicksand, seeking grades and degrees of social value. Other times I waded through domestic quicksand, living as though a secret police unit assigned to enforce housekeeping precision was, at any moment, going to batter down my front door. At home and away, my motives for picture perfect living drove me to follow any directions which professed that such an existence was possible. Consequently, I felt like a pawn of some mysterious social puppet master who orchestrated the flailing in the quicksand. Yet I knew I needed to run free. Once I even wished in written word:

"Although I am proper and responsible and analytical and thoughtful and other good things,

Sometimes I wish I could just enjoy.

I'd like to be carefree and enthusiastic, flexible and optimistic.

I'd like to not think too much about what others think of me.

I'd like to be able to open up instead of close down when life presses in.

I'd like to be able to play instead of work, or just turn work into play.

I'd like to be able to let others know how wonderful they are by simple show and tell, connect with them through just a wave and a smile.

I'd like to be adored, sometimes, and still be respected.

I'd like to 'hang-glide' in life without worrying about the fatality rate, and just once experience the exhilaration of riding off in four directions at once.

Order is nice and necessary, but it isn't usually fun.

I'd like to be able to laugh, even when the joke isn't very funny.

I'd like to be able to tease others without being out of character, and be able to smile when the person being teased isn't pleased.

Most of all, I'd like to be able to love—even without a good reason.

Maybe I can learn."

I desired spontaneity. Instead, I was driven to perfection. In being driven to perfection, I was unable to accept the essence of spontaneity: ambiguity. I could not tolerate the vague, the uncertain, the unplanned, the undefined. In trying to order life precisely, I was destined for failure and unhappiness because life *is* ambiguous. So are people. Uncertainties are just on the other side of every sunrise. As a result, the perfection I sought is impossible to achieve.

Because I insisted on perfection, however, I expected life and everyone in it to cooperate with my plans. I wanted to make a plan and, like a connect-the-dots picture, have life and everyone in it follow the sequence. In my plan, everyone would be detail-conscious and precise.

Life would comply with the lists laid out in my day planner. Everyone would accept that life is serious business and that everything in it should be meaningful. We would all agree that order is more important than almost anything else. As a result of this order, I would be happy because life would be neat and tidy.

Neat and tidy. That was my game plan. I always had a place for everything and everything was put in its place. There was a time for everything, and everything happened on time. I suppose if I had people around me who thought as I did, we would have all marched in time without being aware of differences. But nothing in my life did what I wanted it to do.

With my wonderful husband and beautiful daughter I constantly proposed a structured, traditional format for home life; but since I was "blest" with an untraditional companion and a non-conformist child, try as I might, those expectations remained unmet.

I fell in love with Dallas, my wonderful husband, in large measure because he was happiness personified. In time, however, fun and laughter became less important to me than order, and he was not orderly. Junk from his pockets accumulated on the bedroom dresser, but I knew it was not appropriate for me to clean it up or move it because somewhere in the mound there might be something he considered to be vitally important. He left little stacks of this and that around the house which shouldn't be moved, of course, because he might suddenly want them when I wasn't there and then he wouldn't know where to find them. He loved to cook and, in his way, cleaned up the mess—though he never quite finished the job.

He was disconnected to dates on the calendar: anniversaries, birthdays, and various appointments. I rarely forgot anything and, therefore, thought that he just didn't care. Often he would decide to do things on the spur of the moment and ask me to go along. I usually declined because I had made a different plan, and the plan was paramount to everything else. To make matters worse at those times, he would often go on happily without me.

He seemed to be oblivious to the irritation and frustration I experienced as a result of this disorder, while I simply assumed that my way was the right way and he was just being uncooperative. In truth, he was just living life the way that suited him best. Our personalities, our methodology for dealing with life and relationships (including our own), didn't always mesh well. He was okay with that since he was a believer in individuality and flexibility. I was the one with a problem. I did not understand how he could be so carefree when life was supposed to be serious business.

With so little flexibility and so little understanding of the value of differences, I reached the point where I had a difficult time finding any sunshine while he never seemed to lack for light. I wanted everything to fit in my neat and tidy little universe. I wanted to wind up all the soldiers in my life and have them march rhythmically along. I wanted precision and order before all else. When I was incapable of accomplishing that feat, I ran headlong into stress—and stress pushed me into discouragement. Nevertheless, I refused to give up which only magnified the problem.

My husband's behavior was disorderly enough to provide fertile ground for resentment but, before things got better, they got worse. Teresa joined our family.

I must have assumed, somewhere in my subconscious, that my husband was the odd-ball and that my daughter would, like me, be aligned with order and precision. But while my husband had stacks of stuff here and there, Teresa was like a tornado that left chaos in its wake. She couldn't find anything in the confusion, and neither could anyone else. Where he was spontaneous, she was impulsive and unpredictable. And she was visibly restless in any situation that required her to remain too long in one place focused on, in her opinion, uninteresting things. Being uncooperative seemed to be the primary component in her game plan, if she knew there was even such a thing as a plan. She was so strong-willed that she did not respond favorably to either rewards or punishments.

I finally bought a book titled *The Strong-Willed Child* to see if I could acquire just a little understanding. In the book, author James Dobson compares this type of child to a grocery cart with crooked wheels that simply will not go where you want it to no matter how much effort you exert. (Tyndale House Publishers, Inc.; Wheaton, Illinois; 1978; 20-21.) I had no trouble at all identifying with that analogy.

Just wishing that my family members were more like me, and convinced that life would be a lot better if they were, kept me exhausted. But, in addition, I had constant cultural adjustments to juggle.

My husband was the marketing director for an international company and also served internationally as a mission president and general authority. As a result, we lived in many foreign countries and several places in the United States—from Utah to California to Utah, to Arizona to Missouri to Japan to the Philippines, to New Mexico to Arizona to Colorado to Texas to Canada, to Texas to South Africa to Texas, to Mexico to Spain to Venezuela, to Brazil to Chile. This should have been a wondrous exciting life filled with adventure, and in many ways it was; but for a creature of structure and precision, it was also filled with frustration.

Because I had no spontaneity, the constant differences and adjustments added to my discouragement. Even though, in each location, I eventually created comfort zones where I was at peace, I didn't use the associated lessons in flexibility and adaptation as stepping stones to help with the next challenge. Instead, I coveted my old comfort zone after departure, wanting to return to the familiar, to the place where I had found some order, routine, and understanding.

Our time of sojourn in any strange or foreign location was generally two or three years. Unable to adapt to new things, I always mourned my losses for eighteen to twenty-four months, then I would adjust and find peace for six or eight months, after which we would move and I would start the routine of struggling to accept new cultures, sometimes new languages, and general details all over again. This timing was precise, like a well-rehearsed script, until we moved to Brazil. There I began with my usual mourning, after which I began murmuring and burrowed further and further into discouragement.

Years passed in Brazil: two, three, five, ten. We didn't move and I didn't adapt, partly because I never caught a glimpse of our imminent departure, the "light at the end of tunnel" that had always been my

14

motivation for learning to appreciate a place; but that was not the only problem. In Brazil I was surrounded by 160 million people who all acted like my husband and daughter. If I couldn't value my family, I certainly couldn't value Brazilians. They were disorganized, noisy, happy-go-lucky and, by official polls and surveys, the most optimistic people in the world. In a traffic jam, they could hold a samba festival. If they couldn't rein in their inflationary economy, they would just enjoy the wild ride. Rumor has it that a famous world leader once snubbed Brazil with the comment: "This country is not serious." If he was attempting to belittle the Brazilian attitude, it backfired. Brazilians giggled and chose to interpret his criticism as a compliment.

Since I, like that world leader, was a pessimist, convinced that life should be serious business and Brazilians refused to comply, I was sure they had lost touch with the way life should really be lived on planet Earth. How could I respect, or even be comfortable in a nation that was convinced that life is a party?

Finally the day came when I reached the bottom of the pessimistic pit. I could find no happy thoughts. Grumpy and critical, I had exchanged flexibility for rigidity, personal peace for pretense, personal power and optimism for fear and discouragement, love and mercy for judgment and justice. I had succumbed to the perfectionist

15

philosophies of men, the quicksand, and I had abandoned the great plan of happiness.

I hit the bottom of that pit one day but, miraculously, within twenty-four hours life had literally forced me to do a reality check. On a sunny day in May, in the land called Brazil, I watched the entire population of that nation rise above the grief and sorrow that engulfed them at the sudden and tragic death of their national hero. Ayrton Senna, world-famous athlete, had inspired his countrymen in good times and bad. His successes won their praise, but his sincere love and compassion won their hearts. In their final farewell to him, they poured into the streets by the thousands to cheer his legacy and celebrate his life. As I witnessed their remarkable and powerful tribute, the Spirit whispered that even when all of life seems out of synch, each day can and should be beautiful, joyful.

That day the Spirit began to teach me the gospel—the gospel that had somehow eluded me for several decades in spite of constant church service and activity. This does not mean that I had never, in my half-a-lifetime, tapped into the principles which generate joy. Rather, I experienced them temporarily at various times and recognized their value but, in misunderstanding mortality's realities, I allowed myself to be dragged back into quicksand. In order to break free forever, I needed to replace my doctrinal misconceptions with truth—separate society's unrealistic expectations from the great plan of happiness.

As I began my climb to light, I couldn't help but take notice of the society where I spend most of my time and effort—the church society. As my vision began to clear I could see that, for me and so many others, the secular social emphasis on *more* and *best* was obscuring gospel truth. So often caught up in the focus of conform, compete, and achieve, we march through life as carbon copies of each other in the worst possible way: *a host of stressed perfectionists.*

Although men as well as women are subject to the pull of the quicksand, for currently undefined reasons the quagmire seems to have a more powerful personal effect on women. Perhaps this is because many women often suffer from one of two difficult social paradigms: 1) they are extolled as saintly and put on the proverbial "pedestal," but don't know how to measure up to that ideal; or 2) they are not extolled, in fact are belittled or demeaned and, as a result, don't understand their worth or how to acquire any respect. Men, generally, experience fewer self-image extremes.

While secular culture usually focuses its unrealistic expectations on professional or academic prowess, the focus of the member society is often on home and family—but we still jump into the quicksand.

We scrutinize who has the *most* (children, missionaries, canned peaches, Eagle scouts, temple marriages) and who has the *best* (children, missionaries, canned peaches, houses, ancestors, etc.). Talent at crafts, culinary skills, and related domesticity draws grand applause. A standing ovation is given those who can have their son's Eagle Court of Honor on Thursday, their daughter's temple marriage on Friday, prepare a pantry full of preserves on Saturday, be Relief Society president on Sunday, and graduate from the University on Monday. I don't personally know anyone who ever accomplished such a feat, but I do know we tend to believe that this is a reasonable scenario.

We are caught between two cultures, one bitter and one sweet. We try to blend them together into a palatable lifestyle recipe, but the clash of flavors instead creates conflict. We overlay gospel truth with secular interpretation and, as a result, miss the truth of the scriptures regarding joy and perfection and we can't even hear our leaders:

President Gordon B. Hinckley: "In all of living have much of fun and laughter. Life is to be enjoyed, not just endured" (*Ensign;* © Intellectual Reserve, Inc.; May 1996; 94).

Elder Russell M. Nelson: "Perfection is pending. It can come in full only after the resurrection and only through the Lord" (*Ensign;* © Intellectual Reserve, Inc.; Nov. 1995; 86).

Once I was freed from the power of picture perfect quicksand, not only was I able to separate the bitter from the sweet, I was also able to identify that mysterious puppet master. In a time long ago, he adamantly suggested that forcing us to live in some type of picture perfect quicksand would be good for us. Although his plan of conformity, rigidity, insensitivity, and fear was rejected and he and his troops were subsequently convicted of treason and banished, he has never stopped trying, with sneaky finesse, to sell his miserable proposal (Moses 4:1-4).

Since so many of us these days are buying his line, it has never been more important to understand the truth about mortality's realities.

Mortality Reality:

Discovering the Great Plan

of Happiness

"In this life, I shall have joy..." (Moses 5:10).

I read those words of Father Adam over and over again, trying to focus on their meaning, as the possibilities tumbled around in my mind like the patterns of a kaleidoscope. *This life! Joy in this life!* Surely, Adam knew the truth. Just as surely, I did not. The only hope for me was to discover the same principles he understood—principles that would release me from the relentless social demands and expectations.

And I *knew* that I could find answers because I had received answers before. I knew there was a living prophet. I had a testimony of the Book of Mormon. And I had received direction and guidance for my personal needs at different times in different ways. In seeking release from perfectionism and pessimism, I was certain that help would, again, be available.

Once immersed in desire, with scriptures and research material spread out before me, it did not take too long for me to discover the realities of the fall and the atonement, and the manner in which these events act upon our mortality.

The Fall

I had long known what happened as an immediate result of the fall: Adam and Eve left the garden of Eden and the presence of God to live alone in a world where thorns and thistles grew. I knew that Adam and Eve used their agency and made a choice to enter this world of hardship and tribulation in order to learn good from evil and bring to pass the plan of salvation. I knew that they were not condemned for this decision (Moses 6:53) and, as the second Article of Faith states, neither are we ("We believe that men will be punished for their own sins and not for Adam's transgression"). I knew a lot about the immediate consequences of the fall; but I did not understand what it meant for me, today.

During my studies, in reading 2 Nephi, I began to better understand three particular consequences of the fall:

— Opposition

— Choice

— Inexperience

1) Opposition: In the garden of Eden, there was almost no significant opposition. No good, no bad. No peace, no pain. No happiness, no sadness. That state of no contrast must have been pleasant monotony— like a state of suspended animation. In our hustle-bustle world, it's hard to even imagine such a thing. The only true conflict in the garden was in the presence of two trees: one of life, the other of the knowledge of good and evil. Any other choices in the garden were of no particular consequence: to sleep or eat, to sing or dance, to walk or run. Only in the two trees were there choices of significant, life changing impact. Adam and Eve were told that eating the fruit of the tree of knowledge of good and evil would bring about a radical change of venue: death.

According to Lehi, it is also true that as long as Adam and Eve were in the garden, they would have had no children (2 Nephi 2:23). Children would be a result of partaking of the fruit of the tree of knowledge of good and evil and leaving the garden. Yet they were given two commandments: a) don't eat the fruit of the tree of knowledge of good and evil and b) multiply and replenish the earth. These two directives are in obvious conflict with each other. If Adam and Eve stayed in the garden, they would not have children. To leave and have children, they had to eat the fruit of the tree of knowledge of good and evil. For many people, the question arises as to why they were required to choose between two conflicting commandments. I have always sensed that the need for agency to be represented, even in this situation, required that mortality be brought about by choice, by the use of agency. And in order for there to be choice and agency, there needed to be a conflict in the options available.

When Adam and Eve chose to eat of the fruit of the tree of knowledge of good and evil to bring about mortality and the plan of salvation, opposition became extensive. "For it must needs be, that there is an opposition in all things. If not so...righteousness could not be brought to pass, neither wickedness, neither holiness nor misery, neither good nor bad..." (2 Nephi 2:11). With mortality came an avalanche of pleasant and unpleasant situations. In fact, the tree of knowledge of good and evil was a representation of the reality of mortal opposition: good vs. evil. With such opposition came constant choice.

2) Choice: Only when there are significant consequences does choice become a dilemma. As long as we can either sing or dance and it doesn't really matter which one we choose, there is no confusion in the choice. It is with opposition in choice that we find ourselves conflicted, and it is usually in the choices we make that we discover good/bad, pleasure/pain, etc. We hope to make correct choices. We usually want to do so. And we have our agency. We are free to choose in order that we may gain knowledge. But this opportunity to choose becomes particularly complicated when we realize that we have no experience in making choices in mortality. We often have no idea what we are doing.

3) Inexperience: Because of our inexperience with mortality, we will inevitably make a lot of wrong choices. From academic skills to parenting methods to health issues to neighborliness, we have no experience; therefore, we are usually forced to learn by trial, error, and correction from our own experiences or from the experiences of others. Making a poor choice on any given issue can often be the springboard to making good choices on that issue in the future.

This whole scenario of having major opposition, being required to make hard choices, and often not being certain what to do because of inexperience is, at the very least, frustrating. We don't like feeling so incapable, so weak, so ignorant. We think we should be able to do better on the first try. Unwilling to allow ourselves the necessary practice, we rationalize our behavior and justify our poor choices. We try to appear to be more perfect than we really are because we think we should be. But, in reality, as a result of the fall we are in a situation where we constantly have hard choices to make with no experience.

We sometimes have to choose between obvious good and bad and we still choose bad. Sometimes we must choose between good and good and frustrate ourselves trying to find best.

The reality is that while we are emotionally and psychologically tired from trying to choose perfectly—trying to be perfect—mortality is not a perfect place. It is, instead, a place to learn. But we are impatient. We want to *be* now instead of working to *become.* We will be wrong much of the time even if we are really trying to do right just because that is the nature of mortality: there is opposition in choice and choice without experience.

All of our wrong choices are not sin, which is willful disobedience to things we know are right. Many of our errors are simple mistakes because of inexperience, which inexperience is a result of the fall. Elder Dallin H. Oaks has explained: "Both sins and mistakes can hurt us and both require attention, but the scriptures direct a different treatment. Chewing on a live electrical cord or diving headfirst into water of uncertain depth are mistakes that should be made known so that they can be avoided. Violations of the commandments of God are sins that require chastening and repentance. In the treatment process we should not require repentance for mistakes, but we are commanded to preach the necessity of repentance for sins" ("Sins and Mistakes;" *Ensign;* © Intellectual Reserve, Inc.; Oct. 1996; 62).

The reality of mortality is that it is an imperfect state full of imperfect people. The first step in finding some peace in this is accepting that mortality is a learning experience where we will never learn all we need to know; and, whenever we think we've reached a learning plateau, a new opportunity for trial, error, and correction appears.

I remember a pretest that was given before a university class I took in linguistics. I was starting a new major in speech pathology, having previously been engaged in journalism, history and English. I was pretty good at journalism, history and English, but I had no clue about linguistics and speech therapy. Of the ten pretest questions, I correctly answered none, zero, zilch. I didn't even understand the vocabulary.

I almost ran straight back to the humanities department. It is embarrassing to appear to be so uneducated. But this was a new experience and I needed to learn.

Two years later, degree in hand, I could answer all those pretest questions correctly (and a lot more)—but I had paid a price in trial, error, correction and a huge amount of study and clinical practice. But then I immediately embarked on a graduate program in psychology; and, once again, I had to learn and correct and learn and correct because of my inexperience. One summer, with professor approval, I took an advanced class without the required prerequisite course. The choice to do this created incredible opposition and necessitated unequaled effort. I burned the midnight oil more often than not, met with my professor on a regular basis and, after much trial and error and correction, passed the course with high marks.

Dealing with the consequences of the fall is, for each of us, a lot like those learning experiences were for me. We must give ourselves time to learn—which, it seems to me, is easier to accept in a classroom setting than in daily life.

In my own life, I had such a struggle being happy because I was expecting to be able to create Utopia in an imperfect world—an obvious impossibility. "But," I once pondered, "aren't we trying to create

Zion? Isn't Zion a perfect society? And didn't Enoch succeed?" I now believe the people of Enoch created a society where there was no willful disobedience and where everyone was learning to live by faith, hope, and charity—and doing it quite well. I don't believe anyone in that society could claim perfection—to have eliminated the need for trial, error, and correction and the opportunity to learn and improve on gifts and skills.

Much of our problem with the idea of perfection stems from inaccurate definitions. According to Elder Russell M. Nelson, the word "perfection" in the scriptures is derived from the Greek word *telios* which does not mean to be absolutely correct; rather, it means to be complete or finished, to reach a distant end (*Ensign;* © Intellectual Reserve, Inc.; Nov. 1995; 86). Inherent in this definition of *telios* is the idea of working toward something but waiting for it to be completed. Integrity seems to be implied. Spiritual integrity is to be loyal and steadfast to covenants and commitments. It is to not forsake truth and testimony as we work and wait.

This idea of integrity is the message of a scripture I once found very tiring: "Wherefore, if ye shall press forward, and endure to the end, behold, thus saith the Father: Ye shall have eternal life" (2 Nephi

31:20). By being patiently loyal, there is peace and purpose in "pressing" and "enduring" instead of weariness.

By accepting the realities of mortality that are a result of the fall, we will understand that perfection, completion, is not for now but for a future day.

The Atonement

We are imperfect, living in an imperfect mortality, but there has been One Perfect Person. Through our loyalty, our worthiness, He will one day give us that which we cannot give ourselves: "Come unto Christ and be perfected in Him..." (Moroni 10:32). Perfection will be a gift from the only One who has it to give. In this we find grace, that we are saved by grace—redeemed from the effects of the fall—after all we can do (2 Nephi 25:23). For this reason, we talk of Christ, rejoice in Christ, preach of Christ, prophesy of Christ (2 Nephi 25:26)—and we *must* do so. It is because of the Savior that we can and should have joy.

"Adam fell that men might be; and men are, that they might have joy,

"And the Messiah cometh in the fulness of time, that he may redeem the children of men from the fall. And because that they are redeemed from the fall they have become free forever, knowing good from evil; to act for themselves and not to be acted upon..." (2 Nephi 2:25-26).

Why can we, *why must we*, have "Joy Now" in spite of the struggles, inconsistencies, and imperfections of mortality? *Because the Messiah cometh to redeem us from the fall and make us free!*

Without the promise of the Savior and His atonement, and with all of our mortal imperfections—with all of mortality's realities—as life on earth began there would have been only two choices. The first was to live forever in our sins, which possibility was eliminated when our Father in Heaven kindly made the tree of life inaccessible (Moses 4:31, Genesis 3:24). The idea of living forever in this imperfect world with all of its tragedy and destruction and with all of our personal imperfections and sins is hardly a pleasant prospect. Of course, the other option was worse: living with Satan.

"O the wisdom of God, his mercy and grace! For behold, if the flesh should rise no more our spirits must become subject to that angel who fell from before the presence of the Eternal God, and became the devil, to rise no more.

"And our spirits must have become like unto him, and we become devils, angels to a devil, to be shut out from the presence of our God, and to remain with the father of lies, in misery, like unto himself...

"O how great the goodness of our God, who prepareth a way for our escape from the grasp of this awful monster..." (2 Nephi 9:8-10).

Because of the fall, because of our imperfections, we would be condemned either to this world, which Satan wants to own, or to his kingdom which he already claims. If these were the options, the consequences of earth life proposed in the pre-mortal council, we certainly would not have shouted for joy. But since the plan of redemption was established before the fall, we did shout for joy because we understood these realities of mortality and rejoiced in the fact that our Elder Brother would save us from the obvious and terrible options.

Jesus, Jehovah, The Lamb of God, the King of Kings, the Savior, the Redeemer, the Merciful One, the Mighty God, the Everlasting Father, the Prince of Peace—He would bring to pass the great plan of happiness. He would redeem the children of men from the effects of the fall. His atonement, like a sponge, would soak up our sins upon our repentance, would cover our bad choices, would allow us the practice process of trial and error and correction. Jesus made us free forever because He gave us time and room to work and learn from opposition, choice, and inexperience. He gave us the essential opportunity to live with mortality's realities and still be able to avoid any long term relationship with Satan and his dark kingdom. His mission was, indeed, a rescue mission that would allow us to eventually live forever, with Him, in glory. Knowing He would not fail, we shouted for joy. He would free us from mortality's tragedies, sins, and imperfect practice.

Tragedy: Because the fall brought death and all its attendant weaknesses, illnesses, and inevitable separations, the fall also brought various kinds of pain and loss. Mortality is not located on "Easy Street." Bad things happen to good people, as many victims can attest. Neither righteousness nor isolation can protect us from the challenges, tribulations, and heartaches. Nevertheless, with the great plan of happiness there is no hopelessness. Because of Jesus, there will be reunions and resurrection beyond the veil. The plan of mercy will bring joy in ways unimagined on earth. And even while in mortality, with faith, we can turn to the Savior for comfort. He will make our burdens light, no matter how heavy they seem, if only we can learn how to let go of them and give them to Him.

His goodness stands approved,

Unchanged from day to day,

I'll drop my burden at his feet

And bear a song away.

(*Hymns*, 125)

Sin: When I was young there was a myth being propagated by members of the Church. The myth stated that our life was a like an unblemished board and sins were like nails hammered into the board. Repentance would remove the nails but could not remove the blemishes, the holes in the board, that the nails had made. But Isaiah declared: "Though your sins be as scarlet, they shall be as white as snow; though they be red like crimson, they shall be as wool" (Isaiah 1:18). In truth, because of the atonement and with repentance and forsaking of sin, as the nail comes out the hole is miraculously filled. No trace remains.

"Behold, he who has repented of his sins, the same is forgiven, and I, the Lord, remember them no more" (Doc. & Cov. 58:42).

The Lord forgets, wounds are healed, the holes are filled and the board is returned to its original, unblemished state. Nevertheless, the repentant individual usually retains a remembrance of the entire process. These memories can be blessings that act as a protection from repetition of the sin, although the remembrance does not contain lingering emotional pain. Alma's repentance was complete but he did not forget his sins. He often described them while emphasizing that there was no continuing remorse. Instead, he was filled with exquisite joy at the reality of repentance and the power of the atonement (Alma 36:20).

Even Nephi, who seems nigh unto perfect, recognized the impact of the fall and atonement in his life.

"Nevertheless, notwithstanding the great goodness of the Lord, in showing me his great and marvelous works, my heart exclaimeth: O wretched man that I am! Yea, my heart sorroweth because of my flesh; my soul grieveth because of mine iniquities.

"I am encompassed about, because of the temptations and the sins which do so easily beset me.

"And when I desire to rejoice, my heart groaneth because of my sins; nevertheless, I know in whom I have trusted.

"My God hath been my support; he hath led me through mine afflictions in the wilderness; and he hath preserved me upon the waters of the great deep.

"He hath filled me with his love, even unto the consuming of my flesh" (2 Nephi 4:17-21).

In contrast to Nephi's concluding words of optimism, we often feel hopeless and joyless because the "do it all, be it all" social emphasis of today ignores the effects of the fall and the need for the atonement. In consequence, our focus easily shifts to perfectionism and away from the mortal reality of constant trial, error, and correction.

Imperfect Practice: When I was in the process of learning the importance of trial, error, and correction I often made a checklist of some lessons learned and some lessons still to be learned. One day, as I did so, my list clearly indicated that I had done a good job of conquering negative attitudes and behaviors that I could work on in isolation. I had not done so well with those lessons requiring interaction with others. And the reason for my lack of success was also clear: those learning sessions would be practice sessions and I did not want to make a fool of myself practicing in front of others. Wanting to appear flawless, I preferred to stay in my comfort zone and forfeit the personal progress.

Each day we must work to acquire many new and different skills, and the only way to accomplish this learning is through practice. I had always been so focused on the ideal and so concerned about making mistakes, about the trial and error part of living, that I lost sight of the need to learn and improve. I didn't value the ever-present opportunities for correction and improvement through practice.

Nevertheless, I knew I needed to be more willing to speak up, to take a stand, to try new things, to risk a little and get involved with people and in appropriate causes. But the whole idea made me feel queasy. The prospect of being a spokesperson or being socially assertive was very disconcerting. I simply didn't feel confident of my abilities. Hiding was so much easier.

I tried to find a loophole, a way to learn alone, but there was none. It was very clear that I would only learn by actually doing, making mistakes in the process. Sadly, I was *still* a perfectionist. I needed to accept the reality of trial, error, and correction.

Reluctance to practice had held me back for much of my life. Because I always wanted to appear competent, as often as possible I chose to do things at which I was good and avoided doing things in which I felt inadequate, awkward, or clumsy. A good example is the shadow boxing I did with foreign languages.

In order to learn a foreign language, it is absolutely essential to practice it. And to practice and get feedback generally requires speaking to other people who know the language. And the more practice one gets, the better one learns to use the new structure and articulation. In practicing, however, it is inevitable that the new speaker will make mistakes—lots of them! I remember a friend's story about the first time she gave a short speech in a new language. She confidently plowed through her two or three minute discourse, feeling a sense of supreme accomplishment at the conclusion. Expecting triumphant praise, she asked her husband (an accomplished speaker of the language) to evaluate her effort. He responded with a smile: "You were very enthusiastic. It is, however, the only speech I have ever heard where not one verb was conjugated."

Fortunately, she was not overly sensitive. She learned and she corrected and she did better the next time.

I, on the other hand, was a perfectionist and nothing short of perfection would do. As we lived internationally, I held any foreign language at arms length because I knew I could not speak it perfectly and I was more than reluctant to make the mistakes inherent in practicing. My husband was like my blustery friend who didn't conjugate verbs. He forged ahead in spite of mistakes, learning as he went, unoffended at his own errors or other people's reactions. I always hovered behind, letting him lead the way.

When we lived in Spain, however, I became so frustrated with not being able to interact and have a life of my own that I capitulated and began language study in earnest. I developed my own system for studying language structure and vocabulary that relied on reading the Book of Mormon in English and Spanish simultaneously. This was effective because I knew a lot of words, I just didn't know how to put them together—and I needed gospel vocabulary.

Each day during my personal study time, I wrote down unfamiliar Spanish words in a notebook and listed the English equivalent beside them. If I did not understand a sentence, I analyzed it until I could see how Spanish differed from English in basic sentence construction.

When problems persisted unanswered, I marked them in order to ask someone, in a non-threatening moment, for clarification.

It might be asked why I did not simply get a tutor. First, I was convinced I could develop a better, more individualized study plan for myself than anyone else could—which may have been true. Second, I did not want to practice in front of *anyone.*

Day after day I crept through the reading material and, in just a couple of months, two things began to happen. First, my daily list of unfamiliar words became shorter and shorter. Second, I realized that I was starting to mentally compose some of my thoughts in Spanish. Then, miraculously, I began to speak Spanish in front of others because I knew I had a pretty good level of competency.

I reached my goal: Spanish fluency. But what a long, hard road! How much more fun it would have been to just jump in and practice.

I don't think I'm in a minority in this professed weakness, this pride. We have a society where people want to appear to be practically perfect in every way. At school, at work, at home, in the social scene, we generally do not want to look like we have to practice anything. We want to do things right the first time which is, in reality, rarely if ever an option. Those who will not allow themselves opportunities of trial, error, and correction—opportunities to practice—limit their personal progress, increase their feelings of guilt and inadequacy, struggle with the quicksand, and do not tap into the power of the atonement.

The only way any of us will ever become confident and comfortable with new skills is to practice. But the trial and error of practice rarely, if ever, receives praise. In truth, we need to practice praising practice instead of waiting to only praise perfection. Sometimes we can practice skills privately. Sometimes we must practice them publicly. Either way, we· need to pat ourselves and others on the back for attempting and learning, even if the process itself leaves a lot to be desired.

Miraculously, I learned how to practice. I eventually spoke two or three languages quite imperfectly, and I learned to laugh at my mistakes. I stepped out of my shadowy cave and into the light of living. I tried my hand at new things, went new places, met new people. In spite of my weaknesses, I volunteered for committees and excursions and even a few confrontations. As an added benefit to all these possibilities and opportunities, I found that I no longer tortured myself shuffling between will and will not, do and do not. I gave up indecision. No longer afraid of the mistakes of simple inexperience, I tried to make the best decisions I could without weighing and measuring the possibilities, writing lists of pros and cons, ad infinitum. If I was wrong, I leaned heavily on correction—and a sense of humor.

I was grateful that I was free through the atonement to learn and improve, in my own time and own way. Our Father in Heaven's plan embraces a lot of baby steps, and baby steps are all right. The object of mortality is forward motion, the direction being more important than the speed. But if we are frozen by fear of error, we will never move in any direction, let alone the right one.

Mortality

If we are afraid to try and improve our lives and would rather hide than take some risks and suffer some failures, we can benefit from the lessons taught in the parable of the talents (Matt. 25:14-28).

The parable of the talents in the New Testament is a story about stewardship. A talent in those days was a sum of money, a fairly significant sum of money. In the parable, a man gives his three servants several talents: "And unto one he gave five talents, to another two, and to another one; to every man according to his several ability..." And then the man left on a journey. In the story, the first servant turns his five talents into ten. He that was given two talents increased them to four. But the servant given one talent hid his and did nothing with it. He had only the same one talent to give the master upon his return. The first two servants were commended for their diligence and loyalty, while the third servant was condemned.

Though the parable uses money to explain the principles, and though we often define talents according to the modern day definition of abilities and gifts, the parable does not have just an academic, artistic, or financial focus. Instead, it speaks of the stewardship each of us has over mortal life. The great plan of happiness works with mortality to help us, allow us, to increase our stewardship.

It is important to note that in the parable the initial number of talents, whether five or two or one, is not important. There is no comparison between the servants. The only measure is in what each servant did with what he was given. He with five talents doubled, as did he with two. Though the parable does not specifically state it, there was probably some risk and some failure for these two servants in the learning process—some trial, error, and correction—before increase and improvement were realized. If there had been no risk of any kind, why would the third servant have been so afraid? He was condemned because he was frozen by fear of failure when, to receive commendation, he needed only to increase his stewardship by a little.

Likewise, to be favored or rewarded in our accounting as stewards of our lives, we need only do something good with what we have no matter how much or how little we have in the beginning. Our problems in this process are associated with 1) being like the servant with one talent and letting fear control our progress or 2) believing that unless we 10 times or 100 times our talent, our stewardship, we will not have done enough. With the former attitude we are frozen and with the latter we are stressed. Because of the realities of the fall and the blessing of the atonement, we have the freedom to choose a route somewhere between fear and stress. We can succeed at our stewardships and have peace in the process.

One of our stumbling blocks in finding peace is that the ideal is often taught, and we think we should be ideal, right now, today.

President Joseph F. Smith once said:

"What then is an ideal home—model home, such as it should be the ambition of the Latter-day Saints to build...? It is one in which all worldly considerations are secondary. One in which the father is devoted to the family with which God has blessed him, counting them of first importance, and in which they in turn permit him to live in their hearts. One in which there is confidence, union, love, sacred devotion between father and mother and children and parents...

"Parents...should love and respect each other, and treat each other with respectful decorum and kindly regard all the time. The husband should treat his wife with the utmost courtesy and respect. The husband should never insult her; he should never speak slightly of her, but should always hold her in the highest esteem in the home, in the presence of their children... The wife, also should treat the husband with the greatest respect and courtesy... The wife should be a joy to her husband, and she should live and conduct herself at home so the home will be the most joyous, the most blessed place on earth...

"...nothing should be permitted to come in between you—father and mother, husband and wife; there never should be a shade of difference of feeling; there never should be a thing permitted to come between you and estrange you one from another; you should not allow it" (*Teachings of Presidents of the Church, Joseph F. Smith;* Intellectual Reserve, Inc.; 1998; 180).

After using this quote in a Relief Society class, I found the sisters filled with guilt for not measuring up to this great ideal. I had to re-read to them President Smith's opening statement: "What then is an ideal home—model home, such as it should be the ambition of the Latter-day Saints to *build*...."

President Smith was suggesting principles to work toward. Again, too often we feel a need to be ideal *now* rather than being willing to work toward one day becoming such.

When we understand the realities of mortality, we don't always have to refer to an eternal "to do list" or "measuring stick." We only have to obediently face the right direction and, according to the circumstances of the moment, celebrate the freedom to learn, to choose, to balance, to become—all at our own pace. Yes, there are times when we will be asked or when we will know that we have to stretch more than usual, give all the energy we have and then some, for a period of time. With a proper perspective on the plan and ourselves, coupled with personal inspiration, we'll know how much to give at any particular moment, and we'll have peace and joy.

In short: we can press forward steadfastly and endure to the end because it requires only imperfect mortal effort, balanced effort, not perfect super-human effort. And we can do it with joy because Jesus has compensated for and will comfort us in all of mortality's realities. Because of His rescue mission, the plan is called the great plan of happiness, the plan of salvation, the plan of redemption, the plan of mercy, and other glorious, joyful names. In spite of inevitable mortal challenges, it is never called the plan of justice, of sadness, or of rejection.

Since the plan is so simple, so beautiful, so stress free, what has happened? In looking at my own life I have concluded that we have, indeed, mixed this beautiful gospel culture with a social culture of unrealistic expectations. We have a difficult time interpreting the meaning of "sweet is the peace the gospel brings" because we have managed to turn the great plan of happiness into the great plan of stress. We have done this by aligning ourselves with conformity and precision, with social competition, and with the resulting fearful, judgmental attitudes. To find gospel peace, we must exit the quicksand and exchange the game of competition and precision for mortality's realities of trial, error, and correction. We must turn to diversity and flexibility, to faith and hope, to charity and mercy. These principles are the essence of the great plan of happiness.

BE YOURSELF:

TAMING THE MASQUERADE

"To thine own self be true" (Hamlet, William Shakespeare).

In the "olden days," when I was growing up, I do not remember that I insisted on conformity in others or felt in myself a need to conform. I made my own choices about my activities and educational pursuits, and I did not much care what others thought.

I remember standing, talking, with a group of friends shortly after graduation from high school. They were discussing plans to join sororities and social clubs at the beginning of their freshman year of college. I, quite nonchalantly, announced that I had no intention of joining either. From the reaction of my classmates in the circle, you would have thought I had just said I was going to defect from the United States. I did not even try to explain as, obviously, they would not have understood. I also did not feel a need to re-evaluate my decision. Although most people in those days would have classified me as structured and responsible rather than flexible, unique, and fun-loving, I did a lot of diverse things with a lot of diverse people. Life was good. I liked myself pretty well and I liked all of them, too. I was comfortable with variety.

Then I got married at twenty-something and, somehow, society "conned" me into believing that I needed to match some pre-determined stereotype. I developed the idea that I was supposed to surrender my individuality. Although no one in my immediate vicinity, not even my husband, required that I conform to some social model, the social vibes were strong enough that I got sucked into the masquerade anyway. I often felt guilty if I was detached and independent, if I was less than a "cookie-cutter" wife, if I didn't have the domestic charm of the television "Cinderellas" of that era: Beaver Cleaver's mother, June; Harriet Nelson; Donna Reed; and Samantha Stevens—minus Samantha's magic tricks. In today's TV world, their counterparts would probably be the various domestic divas who conjure up bounteous ways to garnish, with ruffles and flourishes, everything from weddings to picnics.

My bouts with this image dominated my life for ten years. During that time I lived for a while in a small town in the western United States. Because I wanted "to belong," be an acceptable part of the local population, I tried to conform. It was, however, a place where I didn't fit. People there later told me that they perceived me as unhappy, but they insinuated that my dissatisfaction was because I wasn't enough like them. Instead, it was because I wasn't enough of me.

For example, when I arrived there I was an avid football fan (and still am); but it didn't take long for the bread-baking, female village population to make me feel like a strange creature from outer space and, in trying to fit in, I almost surrendered my love of the game (or at least any visible public interest in it) rather than endure their scorn.

I tried to fit into their cultural "box," but it was a very uncomfortable fit. Perhaps I would have continued to try and match their ideal and, therefore, surrendered more and more of myself; but, fortunately, a move to Texas intervened. Once there, all I had to do was change my football allegiance from the Colts to the Cowboys—an easy transition.

I was myself again, but only because I had moved to a place that was a good fit. I still couldn't love myself and be myself regardless of the expectations of people around me. To be a football fan in a bread-baking community and to, at least occasionally, cheer for the Colts in Cowboy country—and to do so just to be me rather than to prove something about independence and non-conformity—would have been the beginning of taming the masquerade.

However, Texas would allow me to be myself for a while.

During that time in Texas, I worked in the world's craziest office with the world's craziest people. For a month or so I looked disapprovingly upon my happy-go-lucky, disorganized office co-workers. But I was there with them every day, all day; and pretty soon I began to laugh at them and, eventually, with them. In a few weeks, I warmed up to their flexibility and spontaneity, their total disregard for a social masquerade. It took another month for me to rediscover who I really was and adjust my attitude, my hair style, and my wardrobe (within tight budget constraints).

Though I loosened up a lot, I wasn't just like them. The real me was too organized and predictable, and I didn't want to forfeit the real me. But I caught their sparkle and it felt so good! I kept thinking that this was a new me but it was really the old me, the real me, come alive again. I accepted my individuality and the individuality of others. I was in love with life.

For five years I was something of an "eccentric," caught up in being myself, and I didn't care who knew it. I didn't need to cheer for the Colts because I was completely converted to the Cowboys. My husband and I had more fun in those years, like we did when we were dating and first married and I didn't feel compelled to conform. I'm sure there are a couple of countries in the world where I have a reputation for being, to put it mildly, different. Now I know that I was simply being myself, totally unconcerned about the masquerade.

But, unknown to me, the masquerade was alive and well, in hibernation.

I remained joyful through two foreign assignments and two return sojourns in Texas, as well as in a surprise move to Mexico that jerked me away from what I thought would be a long- term Texas life and left me with a void and severe homesickness. Nevertheless, I was not hostile to Mexico. I simply missed Texas until, in time, my heart found a home in Mexico. It was only in leaving Mexico, when I was thirty-something, that the masquerade beckoned to me again and I heard and heeded the call.

The impetus for this relapse was an invitation to move to Spain on a new and challenging assignment. My husband had been called to serve as a mission president. We would be leaving the world of business for three years to supervise a few hundred missionaries.

Excited about my idea of Spanish charm, about my involvement in the work, and about the prospect of enjoying meaningful connections with the people, I embarked for Europe with a ream of rosy life-style expectations, including a revitalized premise emphasizing the value of order, solemnity, and perfection. Most unfortunately, I carved out a mental image in concrete of a wholly fictitious model of the role I would fill, the person I would be, to which image I planned to conform. I thought I had long since given up the need to be a clone of the television Cinderellas, but not so. The cookie-cutter mentality awoke from its long sleep and stormed back into my life with real intent when I decided that my responsibilities in Spain would give me the consummate opportunity to become "Super-Domestic-Woman."

How could I have forsaken so quickly everything I had enjoyed for more than half a decade? Why did I again surrender my individuality? In short: I had never completely severed the connection to the quicksand and so, with a push in the right direction, the emphasis on conform, compete, and achieve lured me back. In this case, I was caught in a church culture that had little to do with the gospel.

As the "TV Cinderella" image reawakened, it collided head on with the fact that I had been thrust into the spotlight, in Spain, as a prominent leader of an organization that seemed to trumpet the angelic value of domesticity. Consequently, I falsely concluded that my current duties pre-supposed a focused conformity to a home-style role model. Although I did not have to completely abandon football this time around as it was not an issue of any consequence in the current culture, I was certainly reduced to carbon copy thinking. In seeking to conform, once again I forfeited my real self believing that I was suppose to match a "Cinderella stereotype" when, in fact, my feet wouldn't even begin to fit into her shoes. For me, such a fairytale aspiration carried with it certain discouragement.

Over the years, whenever I allowed myself to be pulled back into a domestic mold, I fell into a black hole of discouragement, even depression, because I was surrendering myself, letting myself be manipulated by society. Although I would occasionally find a way to climb out for a few months or a few years, eventually I would allow society to intervene and I would be sucked back in again. Succumbing to the lure of any masquerade—be it academic, professional, social, athletic, domestic, or some other type—always creates a sense of defeat because it is inseparably connected to a lack of personal control. When we forfeit who we really are, stress easily sets in.

Prior to Spain, my half-a-dozen happy years clearly demonstrated that I found no joy in craft stores, fabric displays, and houseware departments. I enjoyed family life, but I was definitely not domestically inclined. Neither, however, was I particularly career-oriented—perhaps because the professional pathway I had been trained to follow did not provide much personal satisfaction either. But during those years, whether I was a working woman or a stay-at-home mom, I always included some time for my personal interests: studying, teaching, reading, and writing.

In Spain, however, I forgot the importance of being myself and so I deleted the category of "personal interests" from my life adding in its place crafts, cookies, and compulsive cleaning. Before long, I was predictably stressed and depressed.

I initially assumed that this unhappiness resulted from the fact that the country, the work, and the people did not measure up to my rosy expectations—my Utopia. I also thought my discontent might be a consequence of my initial lack of fluency in the Spanish language. I even suggested that I was "out-of-sorts" because the local gentry were suspicious of me. I was not a carbon copy of others who stood in my place previously (although I tried to be), and the resulting competition and comparison left me far behind in the race for approval.

But in truth, if I had only been comfortable with myself, with the value of the real me, I could have been in control of my own happiness. The stress stemmed from the fact that I could not match the perfectly fictitious role model in my imagination of who I should be and, therefore, I did not approve of myself.

One day, many months after our arrival in Spain, having grown tired of the pretense, I decided to go in search of a little of myself again. I stored the craft needles, the cookie cutters, and the cleaning cloths and, in those pre-computer days, requisitioned a typewriter from the office.

I set the writing machine on the dining room table, rolled in a sheet of paper, typed a title, and began to compose.

At first my thought processes were a bit sluggish, having been buried for some time in a mountain of cookie dough, but soon the words began to flow—and a few tears fell as the real me threw off the shackles of non-essential domesticity. Minutes ran into hours, yet time seemed to stand still. My imagination and the typewriter keys painted linguistic pictures of people and places that danced happily across the pages. And I danced with them, finally free.

After that, my search for "Super-Domestic-Woman" ceased. I realized that trying to conform to "angelic domesticity" did nothing to make me feel angelic. I also recognized that the excessive homemaker "hype" to which I had succumbed was not gospel truth. It emanated from a social culture which was dedicated to the proposition that home and family are inseparably connected to cross-stitch and cookies. I was learning that home and family could comfortably belong to personalities quite different than the television Cinderellas.

Although I took that lesson from Spain with me when I left and it helped me find some personal peace, it was not until a decade later in Brazil, when I went in search of the underlying principles of joy, that I was finally able to disengage from the need to do and say things based on the expectations of people in the society around me. And it was about that time that I hung a favorite *Mormonad* on the wall in my office. On the poster is a picture of a tall vase of elegant, long-stemmed red roses with a single sprightly daisy dancing in the center of the bouquet. The caption reads: *Be your own kind of beautiful.* For me, that illustration had to do with more than physical beauty. To me, it said: *Be yourself.*

There is a little fable I have learned to appreciate.

One time the animals had a school. The curriculum consisted of running, climbing, flying, and swimming, and all of the animals took all of the subjects.

The duck was good in swimming. Better, in fact, than his instructors; and he made passing grades in flying but was practically hopeless in running. Because he was low in this subject, he was made to stay in after school and drop his swimming class in order to practice running. He kept this up until he was only average in swimming. But average is acceptable, so nobody worried about that. Except the duck.

The eagle was considered a problem pupil and was disciplined severely. He beat all the others to the top of the tree in climbing class, but he used his own way of getting there.

The rabbit started out at the top of the class in running, but he had a nervous breakdown and had to drop out of school on account of so much make-up work in swimming.

The squirrel led the climbing class, but his flying teacher made him start his flying lessons from the ground up instead of the top of the tree down, and he developed charley horses from over-exertion at the take-off and began getting C's in climbing, D's in running.

The practical prairie dogs apprenticed their off-spring to a badger when the school authorities refused to add digging to the curriculum.

At the end of the year, an abnormal eel who could swim well, and run, climb, and fly a little was made Valedictorian. (Anonymous)

We are not and cannot all be good at everything. We are not all alike. Yet we gravitate toward conformity. I suppose life might be easier if all of us were the same. Then we would all choose to do the same things, at the same time, in the same way, and we would never have to struggle to try and understand why others are different. A case in point is Henry Higgins humorous soliloquy in *My Fair Lady:* "Why can't a woman, be more like a man..."

Differences are the nature of life. We don't all do the same things. We don't all like the same things. We don't all learn the same way. We aren't all at the same place in life's journey. Even so-called identical twins are not exact replicas of each other. To criticize the diversity is useless, and yet we don't seem to know how to live with it.

As President Brigham Young declared: "It floods my heart with sorrow to see so many Elders of Israel who wish everybody to come to their standard and be measured by their measure. Every man must be just so long, to fit their iron bedstead [see Isaiah 28:20] or be cut off to the right length; if too short, he must be stretched to fill the requirement.

"If they see an erring brother or sister, whose course does not comport with their particular ideas of things, they conclude at once that he or she cannot be a Saint, and withdraw their fellowship, concluding that, if they are in the path of truth, others must have precisely their weight and dimension" (*Discourses of Brigham Young;* selected and arranged by John A. Widtsoe; The Church of Jesus Christ of Latter-day Saints; Salt Lake City, Utah; 1977; 279).

In the New Testament, Paul taught about the reality and the value of diversity.

"Now there are diversities of gifts, but the same Spirit.

"And there are differences of administrations, but the same Lord.

"And there are diversities of operations, but it is the same God which worketh all in all.

"But the manifestation of the Spirit is given to every man to profit withal.

"For to one is given by the Spirit the word of wisdom; to another the word of knowledge by the same Spirit;

"To another faith by the same Spirit; to another the gifts of healing by the same Spirit;

"To another the working of miracles; to another prophecy; to another discerning of spirits; to another divers kinds of tongues; to another the interpretations of tongues:

"But all these worketh that one and the selfsame Spirit, dividing to every man severally as he will" (1 Cor. 12:4-11).

Spiritually, we are different. We have different spiritual sensitivities and spiritual gifts. We learn from each other and lean on each other because of our differences; and it's okay if we live the gospel in slightly different ways, for we are at different levels of understanding and progress. Being critical or feeling inferior to those on different levels than we are is to disregard Paul's advice. We are all important and we all need each other.

"...The eye cannot say unto the hand, I have no need of thee: nor again the head to the feet, I have no need of you.

"Nay, much more those members of the body, which seem to be more feeble, are necessary:

"And those members of the body, which we think to be less honourable, upon these we bestow more abundant honour; and our uncomely parts have more abundant comeliness" (1 Cor. 12:21-23).

The gospel teaches diversity—the importance of being your own best self. I once had a note posted on my refrigerator that suggested: "Since God made us to be originals, why stoop to be a copy?"

While obedience is an important gospel principle, conformity is not. Obedience does not require that we forfeit our identity. Obedience is choosing the right and the opportunity to be one in truth and purpose with others through ordinances and covenants while still retaining our individuality, personality, interests, and gifts. Even trying to become like Jesus does not require that we abandon our own selves. Conformity, however, negates innate uniqueness. It requires that we forfeit our identities, even our talents and gifts, in order to all be alike or to be like someone else. This is especially dangerous when the model or mold is formed from a false or counterfeit premise.

Elder Neal A. Maxwell has suggested: "Though [Satan] postures as a non-conformist, my how the adversary likes his lemmings to line up and march—toward self-destruction—to the most conforming cadence caller of them all!" (*Things As They Really Are*; Deseret Book Co.; Salt Lake City, Utah; 1980; 7.)

Whenever I spent my time masquerading, everything seemed so tiring, so impossible. It seemed impossible, of course, because with the incentive of *more, better* and *best,* I insisted on doing everything right and doing everything myself. That masquerade of total independence and pompous self-sufficiency automatically makes everything impossible. The gospel says we can lay our burdens at His feet. Society, however, insists that we do it all and be it all. Because we want to appear flawless, competent, and fit into the molds others perceive as valuable, we live with doubt, fear, and even dishonesty.

During all the years I spent trying unsuccessfully to be someone I wasn't, no one knew I was miserable. I put on a happy face, but there was no true happiness inside. I drifted in and out of the masquerade over many years until finally I found the true joy of just being myself.

After that, I often sensed some of my former challenges in the lives of others. Friends would come to me saying that they could even recognize a visible difference in my countenance, asking me what had happened to bring about the change. Privately, one on one, I shared my past and present struggles as well as principles that had helped me find the freedom. These conversations were with close friends, and I saw light in their souls and tears in their eyes as I explained my new insights. Like me they were stressed perfectionists; and in my story they felt the power, the peace, and the joy of learning to live without the masquerade.

I was grateful I could give them a little bit of vision; but when the opportunity came for me to speak publicly about the subject, I was more than reluctant to share the real me. In fact, I was downright afraid. My audience would, for the most part, be people I did not know. What would they think of me if I admitted I did not have "all my ducks lined up in a row," if I admitted I was still struggling with personal weaknesses and that my life and no one in it worked according to the rules and regulations of the masquerade?

Because of my fears, for my first public discussion on the subject I composed a presentation based on the principles without including my personal story in any detailed way. Then, because I knew there was something wrong with that composition, I rewrote it several times, never including myself in the story until, finally, the insistence of a friend and a personal crisis combined to convince me that I needed to be honest with my audience about my learning experiences, even my weaknesses.

The power of the masquerade had tried to pull me back in with a focus on conformity, perfectionism, and approval-seeking behavior. The war to learn to be myself was not over, perhaps never would be, but I would win this battle.

Fear left as I felt the peace necessary to proceed with a very spontaneous, personalized presentation. Since that time, whenever I have had the opportunity to share my experiences with others I have found that, though the principles of which I speak touch other's lives, the most effective tool I have is honesty about myself. Listeners will often confide to me, "If we would all stop trying to appear to be perfect and just share our fears and sufferings honestly with each other, we could love and support each other better."

If we can just find the courage to shake off the shackles of pretense, dissolve the plastic façade of perfection, we will find those golden nuggets of truth which convince us that it is okay to be who we really are. As an unknown philosopher once observed: "It is only when you don't run from yourself that you begin to get somewhere."

In my case, I eventually stopped running from myself and learned to interact with society differently. Instead of embracing society's focus on rigidity and conformity, I carefully avoided such stressful precision. Nevertheless, I did not become a hermit. Rather, I simply decided to participate in society without allowing it to dictate how I should run my life.

The more I left the masquerade behind, the more I was able to look around objectively and see which aspects of my environment had value for me and which did not. As I disengaged, I learned how to toss out non-essentials. I was no longer society's servant. Instead, society was mine as I accepted only those portions that helped me and those around me find peace and joy and individual progress. Society didn't push and pull at me any more. I pushed and pulled at it, being selective and finding ways to make it work for me instead of against me. This I could do once I understood mortality's realities. Happiness and peace are not a result of being pushed along by the crowd, fitting in and conforming. Rather the joy comes from being your own person, even in a sea of carbon copies, from facing life and being in control.

When I accepted my marriage as valuable in spite of its uniqueness, better at some things, worse at others than all the experts proposed—

When I accepted that my daughter was inclined to be disorganized and unconventional, to "buck the system"—

When I accepted that I could be successful, notwithstanding my many failings—

When I accepted the ambiguity in life and the inconsistencies in people—

Then I had peace. Then I was happy.

My expectations were in line with what was real.

This was not abdication of plans or purpose or truth. It was just rejection of the masquerade, a realization that so much of society's focus, even the church society, is on things that contain no lasting joy— a focus that is so often the product of the quicksand to conform, compete, and achieve with a goal of social approval.

Fortunately, I learned all of this before the day when my identity was sorely tested.

We were living in Santiago, Chile when, shortly after noon on a summer day, I was notified that, during a short fishing trip, my husband had been separated from his fishing float tube and, in the process of swimming the short distance to shore, had disappeared and could not be found. Six long days later, word came that the search was finally over. Hope of finding him alive was gone.

Even though I sensed that he had been called to some new and important work beyond the veil, as the impact of these events on my life became clear, I was caught in the shadows of how much I would miss him: his enthusiasm, his leadership, his friendship, his spontaneity. I was grateful that I had learned to appreciate our differences. Since we were living overseas on a church assignment at the time, I knew I would be moving to a new place, making a new life for myself, finding a new focus in each day. With these thoughts, I suddenly felt my personal identity slipping away. *Who was I now? What was expected? Who would I be?*

But then, I remembered the *Mormonad:* the lone daisy. Although I felt lost and very much alone, comfort and understanding embraced me. I had once learned that I did not need to be a "cookie-cutter" wife. Now I realized that I need not be a "cookie-cutter" widow. I would have much to learn in my new life, but I was still just me and I was still very free!

Be yourself. There are no social molds into which we need to fit. Moses and Aaron were different. Peter and John were different. Joseph and Brigham were different. None of the women in the scriptures were alike. No matter our state or station in life, the pretense of trying to be someone else, someone more perfect, flawless, or socially acceptable is a stressful masquerade. Diversity, not conformity, is part of the great plan of happiness.

Someone Else

by Michael McLean

I am seeing my reflection
Through somebody else's eyes
I can't tell which part is me
And which part is a bad disguise

I am hearing my opinions
Through somebody else's ears
I can barely recognize my hopes
My dreams and all my fears.

I'm someone's neighbor
I'm someone's child and someone's friend
And they see through me
With their own peculiar lens

Why in the World Did We All Shout for Joy?

I'm carving out a place for me

With someone else's knife

Could it be that I am living

Someone else's life?

I am writing my life's story

With somebody else's pen

Think I really need to find my own

And start all over again.

I've got to find out who I am

I've got to find out who I am

Got to know and got to see

What's making me, me

I've got to find out who I am

I've got to find out who I am

And when I do I know

I'll be all I can

When I find out who I am

Got to find out who I am.

(*Safe Harbors;* Deseret Book Co.; Salt Lake City, Utah; 1999)

FINDING FLEXIBILITY:
THE LETTER KILLETH—
SO KILL THE LETTER

"The letter killeth, but the spirit giveth life" (2 Corinthians 3:6).

The phrase "letter of the law," though not confined to ancient history, finds its origins there.

In about 600 B.C., the Biblical kingdom of Judah was carried off captive into Babylon. Prior to this captivity, the people had been unfaithful followers of Jehovah by mingling worship of the One True God with worship of the pagan gods of the surrounding kingdoms. Upon their return to Jerusalem after the captivity, however, they recognized their folly and became zealously loyal but, unfortunately, not loyal to Jehovah. Rather they became totally committed to the written word, the Law of Moses.

In just a few hundred years, the law was dissected, added to, structured, debated, even twisted. The law became the focus, the foundation, the support, the "god." With such apostasy, the Jews began to "look beyond the mark," beyond what was really important. The additions—the stringent, detailed rules and regulations—became more important than the original law, even more important than the God who gave the law.

Since the people had no living prophets, interpretation of the law fell upon the intellectuals and religious leaders who often could not agree. As a result, factions arose, for example: the Pharisees, the Sadducees, the Scribes, the Essenes. They debated fiercely with each other over interpretations of the law. Countless rules were devised as explanations of precise ways to live the commandments, attempting to mandate and control every movement. This structure eliminated the need—even eliminated the desire—for personal initiative, for individual evaluation and application, for the direction of the Spirit. In New Testament times, the phrase "letter of the law" was a linguistic method of referring to the strict Law of Moses and the infinite number of rigid rules and regulations that the Jews had attached to it. When Jesus walked among them He was rejected, in part, because He condemned their "letter of the law" perspectives and lifestyle (see Matt. 12:1-14).

The apostle Paul spent a great deal of his teaching time trying to help the new Church members understand that the "letter of the law" no longer applied—neither the strict Law of Moses nor the rigid additions—that there would be no new "letter." Instead, they needed to learn to live by the spirit—by common sense, love, devotion, and personal inspiration. Perhaps his most famous and fundamental word on the subject is found in 2 Corinthians 3:6, "...the letter killeth, but the spirit giveth life."

Today, "letter of the law" social structure still lives. It can exist anytime, anywhere. Wherever it is found, it kills the joy because it eliminates options and pushes us beyond what is needful and reasonable. It is often bound up in doing that which will bring social approval. If society runs, we run. If society works overtime, we work overtime. If society conforms, competes and wears itself out achieving, so do we. We have not learned that the "letter killeth, but the spirit giveth life."

There is a traditional sociological illustration of two different types of cultures and their contrasting responses to life. One type of culture is "contractual," based in "contracts"—rules, regulations and structure.

The other type of culture is "contextual" which is founded, not on the absence of rules, but rather on over-riding the structure when circumstances warrant. According to a popular example, somewhere out in the middle of the desert, on a very deserted highway, there is a traffic signal. When people from a contractual society approach the light and find it red, they stop and wait until the light turns green before proceeding. When people from a contextual society encounter a red light on that very deserted road, they stop, look both ways and, if the road is clear, they proceed on without concern about the color of the light.

Now, because it is true that contractual societies have difficulty grasping the methodology of the contextual, it is necessary for their understanding (i.e. my understanding) to make the "red light in the desert" scenario more specific, to add detail to the basic facts: You have been driving three hours on a dirt road in the desert. You have not seen one car. Suddenly, and surprisingly, you approach an intersection with a semaphore. The light is red. You stop and wait 20 seconds. The light does not change. You wait 30 seconds, 40 seconds, 50 seconds. Still the light does not change. What do you do? Obviously, you look both ways and go through.

Both the contractual and contextual end up doing the same thing. The contractual does it with more caution and possibly with some duress, while the contextual simply accepts the circumstances and responds accordingly. This is not an example of criminal or negligent behavior. It is just using common sense. Caution is not a bad thing at all but, like vitamins, it can be over used. If we are overly cautious, we may never decide how to proceed. Too much contractual behavior produces people so bound to structure that they cannot adapt and change, even in emergencies. But it is also important to recognize that too much contextual behavior can yield unstable, undependable, overly impulsive people. There must be a "marriage" of the two: enough structure to give focus and enough flexibility to change as situations require.

I once heard that Abraham Lincoln commented, "I never had a policy that I could always apply. I've simply attempted to do what made the greatest amount of sense at the moment." Or as another wise sage observed: "Blessed are the flexible for they shall not get bent out of shape."

I learned the value of flexibility in baby-steps—literally one experience at a time. But it was an article in a Brazilian magazine discussing the "contextual" personality of their departed and beloved national hero that sent me on a search for truth. I realized that I had lived my life with contracts, always getting bent out of shape. I had allowed myself to be discouraged because I really believed that, if I just tried hard enough, implemented enough contracts, I could make Utopia happen. This concept was fixed in my mind and nothing, not even beating my head endlessly against mortality's realities, could change it. The contracts, no matter how non-essential or burdensome, seemed to make sense to me until some wake up call alerted me to the truth.

For example, in those masquerade days I once wrote an invisible contract that read: "Food made from scratch (homemade) is more worthy than food made by a shorter process. I am of more worth if I make food from scratch. I will feel guilty when I take a shorter route." Though no tangible copy of this contract was ever in existence, it was just as valid as if it had been signed and notarized.

I had a friend who described her kitchen skills by saying, "I don't cook, I remove box tops." That statement was about as close to my own cooking style as any I had ever heard and I found myself thinking, "I wish I'd said that!" Even if I had, however, there would have been a significant difference between her attitude and mine for the mode of preparation wasn't important to her. She was content. She did not have an invisible "down-home-cookin'" contract. Her family got fed and that was the bottom line. I, on the other hand, felt that the "box top method" was a second rate way to provide food for the family; and, if I was ever to be a first-rate homemaker, I would have to do more "down home cookin'." Ironically, this was my belief even though I intensely disliked every minute I had to spend in the kitchen.

Because of my resentment of culinary duties, I always took short-cuts: letting savory sauce simmer twenty minutes instead of the pro-scribed two hours; mixing one minute on high speed instead of three minutes on low; using easy biscuit mix, pie crust sticks, packaged gravies, and bottled chili sauce—and daily thanking the magicians at the Pillsbury and Betty Crocker kitchens.

Shortcuts got me quickly out of the room in the house I hated most; but because I believed these shortcuts were some sort of transgression, I felt guilty in the recesses of my mind where the "down home cookin'" contract lived and daily did battle with my hatred for the kitchen.

Incredibly, this opposition was only within me. My family never clamored for homemade staples and freshly baked treats. Except on Thanksgiving and Christmas they were quite content with packaged casseroles, microwave popcorn, and store-bought cookies. The contract alone was pushing me and making my life miserable. In my attempts to become "first-rate," I had proven that I could conjure up quite a few "down-home" things, but I did it very seldom and so I continued to feel less than adequate.

Relief from the conflict finally arrived in a magazine article by an author who had a very simple philosophy. As I remember it, she said: If you get your kicks from domestic duties, by all means jump in and enjoy. If you don't, find a way to skim through what has to be done so you have time to indulge in your favorite things. If you want time with the children, stuff everything in the closet and go to the park. If you want to entertain but don't want to clean, knock off the top layer of dust in the living room, dim the lights, and close the doors to the rest of the house. If you don't like to iron, buy permanent press. If you find house-work absolutely intolerable and your home becomes an unrecognizable mess, you can do a major renovation which is creative and quite rewarding. And if you don't like to cook, modern day miracles have made slaving over a hot stove unnecessary.

WAIT! What was that? I blinked, read the pertinent information again, then I shouted for joy! It was okay to pop box tops! The war was over. Something in the novel approach of that article turned on the light in my mind and vaporized my "down-home-cookin'" contract. There were other domestic things I liked to do and lots of non-domestic things. There were other "gifts" I could give my family besides "down-home-cookin'." The contract was not a binding rule. To write the contract at all was inappropriate considering my attitude about kitchen duties. To hang on to it for years was really fool-hardy.

With the contract gone, so was much stress and pessimism. I had been evaluating my value, my self-worth, by my cooking. What a relief to know I didn't have to carry that load! While it is nice to know how to bake bread and can peaches, even if I never did bake and can I could still be worthwhile and charming.

The "down home cookin'" contract was only one of many in my "itsy-bitsy contract" file. I felt safer with lots of contracts at my fingertips that detailed how to execute every minute of every day. This way I was sure life was under control and Utopia was only a short jump away.

No wonder I was stressed and depressed! Utopia only exists in old TV shows like "Father Knows Best" or in the "happily ever after" world of Cinderella. Seeking for such an ideal mortal existence is like being in a race that never ends because, just when you have things in order and feel close to the finish line, someone moves the tape.

To reach for self-improvement is always proper. To mandate impossible, unnecessary objectives is another story. Certainly to tear up the non-essential contracts that are unreasonable and unworkable is just good, common sense.

So often I complained about the rough road I was traveling through life, wondering why I couldn't seem to find life's freeway. Once I learned the truth about mortality's realities, I realized that the map for life does not include a freeway. What a difference that made in my stress level! Discarding the never-ending search for Utopia is liberation. We will be exhausted as long as we think that a perfect existence will come into being if we only try harder, exert more control, apply more discipline, and demand that the ideal materialize. Even though we have to always reach higher and believe we can do better, we also have to accept that "Utopia" is the ultimate unrealistic expectation. We cannot resent life or the people in it when they refuse to do what we have decided they should.

It seems to me that we slip into letter of the law behaviors because of the trilogy of the fall: opposition, choice, inexperience. When we use a letter of the law perspective, we are trying to minimize the opposition, narrow the choices, and compensate for our inexperience. We try to structure the possibility of something nigh unto Utopia. In doing so, we forget that the plan already has us covered, has compensated for our mortality. Since opposition, choice, and inexperience were fundamental to the great plan of happiness, it follows that spontaneity, flexibility, and inaccuracy were also included. All the imprecision is taken into account and covered on a minute to minute basis by the atonement. We are free to live by the spirit that giveth life rather than the letter which killeth through non-essential demands and unrealistic expectations.

When I finally understood this, I felt that my letter of the law lifestyle had actually been negating the daily power of the atonement in my life, diminishing my opportunity to learn and improve. Living by the letter once killed the joy in Israel. In my life, it had certainly killed my joy. Changing to living by the spirit was a little scary, but in it I found a wonderful world. I made lists but I deviated from them often, and I fell asleep at night with a smile on my face even though I hadn't finished all tasks. I stopped trying to insure that, should I die in the next few hours, there would be no items remaining on my "to do" list. I stopped downsizing and upsizing based on the most recent polls and, instead, based a move in any direction on common sense. I stopped running, and I stopped worrying about whether any upwardly mobile maneuvering neighbors would think I was slacking off.

One year, as I was learning to let go of the need for perfectly exe-cuted plans, I was visiting in Utah when a chemical spill on the I-15 freeway stopped and then re-routed all traffic through central Utah. As I watched the news, I imagined the following "detour" scenario:

Sam was heading north on Interstate 15. He had been away more than a week and was looking forward to being in Salt Lake City by dinner time. His wife would have dinner ready and he could visit with the kids before they went to bed. His big rig was streaking along, just barely over the speed limit, making excellent time.

Suddenly he saw miles of cars ahead, all stopped dead still. No one needed to tell him that his dream of being home for dinner would not become a reality. With a sigh, he slowed the truck and brought it to a halt at the end of the long line of cars in the middle lane. He slid from the cab and looked for someone to question about the circumstances. The driver of a white pickup in the inside lane said that a truck carrying dangerous chemicals had apparently overturned on the freeway. No traffic was being allowed through.

Sam, murmuring and grumbling, climbed back up into the driver's seat. Minutes ticked away: 15, 30, 45. Finally, the mass of vehicles began to move, ever so slowly. Sam had an upset stomach, a headache, and a nervous tick at the side of his mouth. He hated delays, he hated detours, but it seemed he had no choice. All traffic was being diverted to the old highway, through a dozen little towns. Sam sputtered and muttered. He wanted to step on the accelerator and race on home. Instead, he would have to crawl along with everyone else. He hated traffic. He hated little towns. He hated two lane roads.

Sam was hungry, but stopping to eat would waste time. The hungrier he got, the worse the trip became, and the more he hated everything. He drove on, seeing nothing but a big black cloud; and when he was finally able to turn onto the freeway, he even cursed it.

Arriving home, he yelled at his wife and didn't say a decent word to his kids for three days. Blast that chemical truck, anyway. It had ruined his life.

Sam had lots of little contracts about the way he expected life to unfold and he didn't handle it well when his contracts were not honored. He refused to look at options, examine some alternatives. Sam eliminated any joy and peace in his life with inflexible rules and expectations. The story could have had a different ending.

Sam was heading north on Interstate 15. He had been away for more than a week and was looking forward to being in Salt

Lake City by dinner time. His wife would have dinner ready and he could visit with his kids before they went to bed. His big rig was streaking along, just barely over the speed limit, making excellent time.

Suddenly he saw miles of cars ahead, all stopped dead still. No one needed to tell him that his dream of being home for dinner would not become a reality. With a sigh, he slowed the truck and brought it to a halt at the end of a long line of cars in the middle lane.

He slid from the cab and looked for someone to question about the circumstances. The driver of a white pickup in the inside lane said that a truck carrying dangerous chemicals had apparently overturned on the freeway. No traffic was being allowed through.

Sam sighed, smiled, and started up a conversation with the driver of the pickup who was also in a hurry to get home. They passed the time talking of trucks and fishing and family and the local news. Suddenly, the mass of vehicles began to move. Sam was surprised to see that 45 minutes had passed. The two drivers waved farewell and scurried back to their vehicles.

From the perch in this cab, Sam could see that the traffic was not being allowed to move ahead on I-15. Instead it was being detoured onto the old highway, through a dozen little towns. Stop and start driving was hardly his favorite way to travel but, since there seemed to be no option, he might as well make the best of it.

In the first town he stopped for a quick hamburger and called his wife. "Don't wait up," he advised. He pulled into a city park to watch the sun set; filled up with gas at a mom-and-pop station; and bought a tall, cool lemonade from some kids with a little stand by the roadside. Between towns four and five, he helped a lady fix a flat tire; and at town number seven, he stopped at an old fashioned candy store and bought his kids some salt-water taffy.

He enjoyed the sights and sounds of small town America so much that he didn't even keep track of the time and when he was finally able to turn back onto the freeway, he flipped on the radio and sang along to the music at the top of his lungs.

For days afterward, he shared his detour adventure with others; and when family vacation came around, they all went back to see where Dad had so much fun the night the Interstate was closed.

There are too many of us who, like Sam #1, insist that life go in the direction we want it to go—or else!! Or else what? Or else we will get all "bent out of shape" because we have a little confusion on our hands? In the end, all we get for that is a case of nerves and a bad headache. Demanding that life comply with our wishes is not an available option. Nothing about life is predictable. Part of living by the spirit is being able to change gears as needed.

Time and time again, one particular Biblical account reminded me of the problems inherent in living by the letter but, because I was so reluctant to deviate from my plans for perfection, I kept being drawn in despite the truth and lessons learned from that story. Those short five verses in Luke tell of a day when Jesus visited with Mary and Martha (Luke 10:38-42). This is the way I have seen that event in my imagination.

Oh, how she loved Him. And because she loved Him she wanted everything to be perfectly prepared. But there had been so much to do that when He arrived many details were still unfinished. The bread was half-baked, the fruit wasn't washed, the serving table wasn't set. She knew she had spent far too much time cleaning the house, but she would not have been satisfied with less, and she had made the trip into the village to buy the best fruit and the vegetables for the soup.

She could have, probably should have, asked her sister to do some of the chores, but Mary was teaching the children who lived next door; and Martha didn't really mind, for the house and kitchen were her realm. She was well-known in the village for her tidy home and her good cooking. Besides, when a special guest was coming, she preferred to take care of the preparations alone.

This day she selected the fruit so carefully that even the vender had become impatient. Each choice needed to be unblemished, plump, and juicy. Finally with a full basket, she rushed home, combed the summer-wind tangles from her long brown hair, put on a cheery yellow tunic and hurried to the kitchen to ready the bread for the oven.

He arrived early. When Mary saw Him, she quickly returned home and eagerly settled herself at His feet. Mary: the teacher, the student. Teaching and learning, never thinking of the damp wisps of hair that needed to be combed into place. Never thinking of the unwashed fruit, the unset table.

As He and Mary sat talking, Martha hustled about feeling jealous emotions rise within her. She wanted to be near Him, too, but first everything had to be completed. Mary could have at least volunteered to help. Martha could have chosen to tell her no. But Mary just sat, intently listening.

So Martha blurted it out, asked Him to reprimand Mary, feeling certain He would see the need for Mary to be concerned about the meal. Instead, He had quietly counseled Martha. And, oh, the sting in His words.

"Martha, Martha, thou art careful and troubled about many things. But one thing is needful, and Mary hath chosen that good part which shall not be taken from her." Martha was stunned. She hurried to the kitchen to weep, but only for a moment. She didn't want Him to see her tears.

She stepped outside, took the bread from the earthen oven and set it aside to cool. Then she washed the fruit and carefully sliced the cheese, each slice a precise copy of the last. That done, she spread the serving table with a blue linen cloth and poured the deep red wine. Finally all was in place including the special sweet tarts baked early that morning. She was pleased with her work.

He had eaten something of each food, always commenting favorably on its appearance and flavor. Afterward, Martha cleared the table hoping He would stay awhile; but only a few moments after she finally sat down beside Mary, He said He must leave. She felt tears forming and quickly blinked them away.

He rose to go. Mary thanked Him for all she had learned. He thanked them for their hospitality and stepped through the doorway into the sunlight. Then He turned back, and His eyes held Martha captive. They read her mind, her heart. Although He did not speak, she heard His words again:

"Martha, thou art careful and troubled. But one thing is needful." Suddenly her tears were set free. He gently touched her damp cheek, then He was gone.

It was late now. Moonlight flooded the doorway. Martha stood there where His eyes had read her mind and His hand had brushed away the tears. She prayed that He would return soon for in the past few hours she had begun to understand. Certainly the preparations were necessary but the shopping could have been done the day before. She could have cleaned the house less meticulously. She could have sliced the cheese less precisely. Early in the day, she could have asked for Mary's help.

It was time to change the priorities in her life for He had said, "One thing is needful."

She did not intend to abandon her reputation as an exceptional cook, neither did she desire to live in an untidy house, but she knew now that the house and the food were less important than the words He had spoken, and she had not taken time to listen.

A breeze drifted by catching the corner of her tunic and she realized that the sun would soon be peeking over the horizon. She hadn't noticed the time passing and did not feel tired. She was waiting for Mary to awaken so that she could ask her to relate all He had said.

And when He came next time, she promised, she would be there at His feet beside Mary. Next time she would listen to Him, learn from Him.

Next time.

Now, I know very little about the customs of the meridian of time, and I know that this story has many different layers of meaning, many different truths that can be revealed to us depending on our needs. Included among all the meanings, however, is a study on the letter and the spirit. Martha was living by the letter and, while food service is certainly appropriate and appreciated, a little less serving at that moment would have been better. The culinary details took control of Martha's life and the resulting stress did not allow her to stand back and analyze the context of the circumstances, determine the priorities of the moment. In her limited "stress perspective" she became insecure, pessimistic, hostile, and judgmental. She reacted emotionally and completely lost her balance, fully expecting that the Savior would support her lopsided view.

I believe she did learn from the experience, however, for the next time we meet Martha, she radiates spontaneity, optimism, and love (John 11:18-28).

The basic problem with me and so many other "Marthas" is that we make "perfect" plans and want them precisely completed. We keep checking off lists and forging ahead with pre-determined mind-sets, even when those lists and mind-sets are no longer valid. *Spontaneous, adaptable, flexible* are words we do not understand. We do not realize that the spirit giveth life.

This is certainly not suggesting that we should avoid goals, objectives, and essential contracts. These can all be valuable tools in focusing our efforts and raising us to a higher level of performance. The danger is in the way the contracts are written.

Any contracts founded in too much perfectionism or idealism should be suspect and subject to revision. Lists and qualifications for ideal jobs, perfect mates, ideal children, perfect home life, ideal educational options should be considered poetry at best, set to music and sung to a wistful heavenly melody, but never expected to be played out in daily life.

Appropriate goals can be nullified by taking on inappropriate details. A goal "to do my best in school" is noteworthy, but the specific need to be an honor student could create unnecessary competition and stress. For parents to expect their children to be successful in individually chosen professions is a wish of appropriate proportions. To streamline it to include only those professions the parents value is to eliminate individuality. To decide to exercise every day possible is workable. To get "bent out of shape" if the feat is not accomplished by 8 a.m. each and every day does not take into account the twists and turns of life.

Competition and comparison can be big problems in setting objectives. "My daughter's wedding must be as elegant as the neighbor's daughter's wedding" would be more realistically rendered: "My daughter's wedding will be as lovely as her wishes and our circumstances will allow." "The neighbor family always looks thus and so, therefore our family must always look thus and so" is a surefire contract for stress.

At church the trend continues. The goal to serve an honorable mission is commendable, but adding that an honorable mission includes being an assistant to the president invalidates the goal in several different ways. On Sundays, we check to see what others are wearing and wonder what other people think of our temporal and spiritual state. Too often we scrutinize the temporal and spiritual states of others. We demand quiet behavior of our children and load them up with guilt and shame when they don't comply. The prodigals—and they are everywhere—are not welcome because, well, what would people think?

In striving to appear that we have, indeed, been able to create a Utopia, a perfect and ideal state, we have instead created stress. And that is not the gospel. While the gospel "giveth life," a letter of the law approach confines us to constantly struggle with things of little import in the eternal scheme of things.

Satan must gleefully watch our scurrying attention to itsy-bitsy contracts while the more essential matters, especially people, go unattended. The story of the good Samaritan seems to say that the Priest and the Levite had some safe but uncompassionate non-involvement contracts, whereas the Samaritan was flexible enough to follow the needs of the moment and the direction of the Spirit. Serving others is almost never convenient and, therefore, requires a contextual, spirit of the law attitude.

Our world of competition and over-achievement makes it difficult to accept the need to downsize great expectations; but if we wish to incorporate the gospel of joy in our lives, at some point we must make a choice to accept mortality's realities. With the trilogy of opposition, choice, and inexperience as our drumbeat, we will probably spend a lifetime arranging and rearranging our great expectations. And that's okay. It's how we learn and improve.

Adam and Eve knew this. They didn't get all bent out of shape because life threw them a few curve balls.

Joseph was sold into Egypt and ended up in prison without justification; but, in living by the spirit, he always did what made the greatest amount of sense in the moment.

Rebekah turned on a dime and, with a smile, packed up her things and went to marry Isaac.

Today, we're often less able to deal with surprises and detours. Schedules, agendas, and plans so often become our criteria for success. We have difficulty accepting that life is a place of constant interruption and necessary change that requires the inclusion of flexibility, options, and exceptions to the rule.

New Year's resolutions are often good examples of simple "contracts" that could use a little downsizing, a contextual approach. Sister Afton Day penned some New Year's resolutions one December 31 in an idealistic, unrealistic, state of mind (*Ensign;* © Intellectual Reserve, Inc.; Jan. 1981; 58-59).

"I will supply my husband's wants and needs with a sweet spirit."

"I will not become distraught with my children."

"I will have my visiting teaching done by the fifteenth of each month."

"I will lose twenty pounds."

"I will not get behind on my laundry."

Not long after, having been untrue to all her good intentions, Sister Day wisely re-wrote the contracts.

"On New Year's Day, I will stock the house with piles of sandwiches and gallons of milk [for the family football fans] and take my daughters to a movie."

"I will forgive my children when they drive me up a wall— and hope they would extend the same courtesy to me."

"I will not ask to be released from visiting teaching, no matter how quickly the calendar creeps up on me."

"I will not gain twenty pounds."

"I will take my husband and children on a tour of the house and show them where I keep the washer and dryer, just in case of emergency."

And she added one new one:

"I will appreciate what little progress I make, despite my shortcomings."

Now that is a plan for happiness!

To reach for self-improvement is always proper. To mandate impossible, unnecessary objectives is another story. Certainly to give up unrealistic expectations and tear up any "contracts" that are unreasonable and unworkable is just good, common sense.

One of the most famous contractual personalities, at least in his theater persona, is Captain Von Trapp of the Austrian Trapp family singers who were made internationally famous in the production *The Sound of Music.*

The Captain, a widower and a military man, ran his family like a naval regiment. Everyone dressed a certain way, behaved a certain way, did his or her duty a certain way, spoke (or did not speak) a certain way. No deviations were allowed. No frivolity was allowed. No exceptions were allowed. The Captain ran a tight ship and everything ran like clockwork. Predictably, however, no one was very happy.

Enter then Maria, a very contextual person. If the sun was shining, tasks were abandoned for the beauty of the meadow. Frivolity and deviations were always appropriate depending on the circumstances. A novice at a Catholic convent, her spontaneity worried and perplexed her associates. She was enough to drive all the contractual sisters at the convent crazy. And so, when a request for a nanny came from one Captain Von Trapp, Maria was selected.

If Maria had created confusion at the convent, she was just about to cause total chaos for Captain Von Trapp. Appalled at the regimentation in his home, Maria quickly made play clothes for the children, took them on outings, taught them to sing, and encouraged fun and laughter. Joy slipped in without warning because spontaneity replaced unnecessary rigidity and the needs of each situation replaced contracts. Everyone suddenly felt very joyful and free—except the Captain, of course, who felt like he was losing control.

Nevertheless, the contractual Captain would begin to loosen up as he fell in love with contextual Maria.

But even Maria had her contracts, and not frivolous ones. She had determined to become a nun. How could she justify her feelings for the Captain? Afraid of losing her identity and making a terrible mistake, she fled to the convent. There an understanding Reverend Mother explained that while the vows of a nun are sacred, so is the love between a man and a woman. Maria then understood the choices in the context of the situation. She decided who she really was, made her decision, and returned to the Captain.

After that, they united their family with faith, hope, and love. They followed their hearts rather than the demands and expectations of society. They made decisions based on truth and the context of the situation.

Contextual, flexible behavior seems on the surface to be disorderly, can even give a sense of abandoning goals and destinations, but it only seems this way to the person who is bound to contracts and great expectations. Captain Von Trapp didn't become disorderly by relaxing his letter of the law contracts. He only became more loving and compassionate. Order is certainly commendable for the word occurs over and over again in the scriptures, particularly the Doctrine and Covenants; but order is not the same as contractual commitment to unrealistic expectations. Order does not mean we should abandon common sense or flexibility.

The scriptures seem to identify several aspects of order, for example:

1) Organizations or groups of people who are united under some specific banner such as an order of the priesthood or the United Order. A family group sheet or pedigree chart represent an "order" that can be translated into people who are organized together in a special (family) group and, therefore, have a specific banner or purpose (Doc.& Cov. 104:1, 107:3, 131:2).

2) Order implies a method for interaction among the members of the organization that is called an "order," This eliminates contention and allows for the proper interchange of ideas and perceptions as the "order," the organization or group, plans and carries out its work (Doc.& Cov. 88:119, 122).

3) There is a sequence to personal progress. It is line upon line, precept upon precept. We cannot get the cart before the horse. In the gospel, there is sequence that must be followed: baptism before endowments, endowments before temple marriage, etc. Life has sequence, too, because childhood comes before adulthood, morning comes before evening, basic math comes before calculus. These kinds of sequences can't be shuffled (Doc. & Cov. 20:68, 130:9, 132:8).

4) There must be a specific adherence to the laws of God. We are not free to develop our own interpretations or consequences (Doc. & Cov. 107:84).

5) It is important to provide for careful preservation of official records (Doc.& Cov. 127:9).

6) We need to allow each person in a meeting or classroom the opportunity to speak while others listen "that all may be

edified of all, and that every man may have an equal privilege" (Doc. & Cov. 88:122).

Order does not appear to mean that our closets, our desk drawers, our agendas and journals will come under spiritual scrutiny, or that our daily lives require a certain type of structure. Even Doctrine and Covenants 90:18, "Set in order your houses; keep slothfulness and uncleanness far from you," may have more to do with spiritual matters than with temporal concerns. Each of us has our own way of organizing personal things and carrying out personal responsibilities, even different ways of defining relationships. There are many ways to carry out these individualized aspects of life.

None of us will receive any eternal commendation for immaculate household or office organization, no matter how praiseworthy society sees it. Every time I visit a certain friend of mine, she has to clear a pathway to the sofa and unclutter the sofa itself in order for us to have a place to talk. I know she will never be judged by the state of her living room, which is clean but cluttered. Rather, her eternal trademark will be the goodness and joy that live abundantly in her heart.

But, even knowing these truths, I am still too often a creature of socially acceptable order. It must be in my DNA. Nevertheless, I have learned to allow something less than perfect order in my domain because straightening things can literally take twenty-five hours a day. Life is so much more than tidiness. I no longer apologize or feel uncomfortable if guests arrive and some things are visibly out of place. I don't have every paper, every spoon, every shoe, every comb and brush neatly tucked away as I once did; and I stopped trying to demand my kind of order from other members of my family.

I traded great expectations of perfect order for joy. It was the best deal I ever made.

In living by the spirit of the law we will gain "life"— joy, passion, excitement. We'll celebrate more and risk more. We will press forward steadfastly without exhaustion. Living by the spirit lets us relax, enjoy, slow down, be imprecise, communicate, share feelings, allow others their own thoughts and individuality. Living by the spirit relieves unnecessary guilt because it allows us trial, error, and correction.

When we live by the spirit, we'll have more family home evenings and fewer family home meetings. We'll sense how to serve sufficiently without running faster than we have strength. We'll focus positively on people, ourselves included. We'll make decisions and act on the needs of the moment instead of on some pre-established and inappropriate "contracts." The letter killeth because it requires a precision that mortality cannot provide. The spirit giveth life because it allows us the opportunity to leave stress behind.

I have learned that, for myself, it is good to set minimum and maximum goals. For example, I have a fifteen minute exercise routine and I have a fifty minute exercise routine as well as a couple in between. These are big and little contracts of a sort from which I select depending on the context, the situation. And, even though I often wish to do more of everything, I have concluded that wishing and guilt do not need to walk hand in hand.

Sometime after I began to "loosen up," I heard a commentator on a news program suggest that many repressive societies are repressive because they have a "fear of chaos." They believe things will spin out of control if they don't wield a heavy hand, mandate order, command in all things, keep everyone and everything in the proper place.

So much of society seems to adopt that stance, just as I once did, proposing that we should be able to make life and people consistently cooperate, follow our plans, complete our "connect-the-dots" pictures, and conform to our itsy-bitsy contracts. But this letter of the law focus is truly similar to the plan invented by the other guy in that pre-mortal council, the puppet master, the one who "wants his lemmings to line up and march toward self-destruction." Such inflexibility cannot incorporate agency and has no place in the great plan of happiness.

Paul was, of course, correct: "The letter killeth, but the spirit giveth life." For our own peace of mind, we must kill the stressful letter, reject unrealistic expectations, and get into a different, more flexible, more optimistic frame of mind.

FAITH AND HOPE:
FRAMES OF MIND

"Be not afraid, only believe" (Mark 5:36).

During my years of living by the letter and masquerading, I was the kind of person who liked to cuddle up to my comfort zone, a warm and cozy place of well-known proportions. In the winter, it included a crackling fire and a good book; in the summer, it was a sun-drenched beach and a good book—both in isolation. As long as I was by myself, I could keep most things orderly. People tend to add chaos, unpleasant weather, to the scene.

I suppose it's odd that I would be so inhibited considering the number of times I found myself moving on to new and unknown places with strange sounding names. But no matter where I was, I always hoped to find a good book and the equivalent of a crackling fire or a sun-drenched beach. Wherever in the world I was, I could cuddle up to a book and almost forget that chaos waits to pounce. In my cozy place, I could also set aside my perpetual bad attitude—which was often a result of moving on to new and unknown places with strange sounding names.

When my husband was asked by his employers to move to Mexico, we were living in Texas near corporate headquarters. We lived in Texas three different times, each stay interrupted by international assignments. On the third and final return there, we really "settled in." I returned to university studies, completed my bachelor's degree, and was accepted into graduate school. I had a group of associates who were truly numbered among my best friends. At church, I was called to work with my favorite people, the young women. We had a medium-sized sailboat with sleeping facilities on a lake a few minutes from home; and, for the first time, we actually had our very own home, a small but comfortable condominium. I only agreed to the transfer to Mexico because I felt certain that, if I did not go, one day I would regret the lost opportunities. Nevertheless, the thought of moving and letting go of Texas was almost more than I could bear.

And, as expected, the transition to Mexico was difficult. In leaving Texas, I was leaving a comfort zone of incredible power. Not only didn't I want a new one, I didn't know how to create one. I cried intermittently all the way to Mexico City, feeling acutely aware that it would be a long time, if ever, before I would live in Texas again. I compared the void I felt in Mexico to the warm blanket that was Texas, and Mexico came up short. It did not seem to matter that we had a pleasant apartment, that I found a way to do some post-graduate studies by correspondence, that I was again called to teach young women, or that almost everyone on our correspondence list came to visit and I was fortunate to be the unpaid tour guide. At least, it did not matter in the beginning as I refused to let go of the old comfort zone. With my mind-set, the familiar past was much more alluring than the fearful unknowns of the future.

A year-and-a-half after arriving in Mexico, I went back to Texas for a month to follow-up on some course work at the university. For twenty-seven days in Texas, I was in heaven. Then, standing in the library between stacks of books on educational psychology, an invisible lightning bolt struck and I knew clearly that Texas was past. I had to go "home" to Mexico and look ahead. In that moment I let go of wishes for the past, began to look for good in the present, and exchanged the old comfort zone for a new one. Before long, I fell in love with Mexico: the people, the history, the teaching, the touring. I would have willingly stayed there forever had we not been asked to move to Spain.

When the day to depart Mexico arrived, a group of friends came to the airport to see us off. As we tearfully waved goodbye to them and simultaneously and reluctantly relinquished our Mexican residence visas to the curious immigration official, Dallas explained our obvious emotional state in Spanish: *"Los que piensan que es fácil decir adiós nunca han tenido que decir adiós"* ("Those who think it's easy to say goodbye have never had to say goodbye").

Because it was not easy to say goodbye, the lesson from the university library was soon forgotten. From it I should have learned to let go of the pull of the past and fall in love with the next opportunity, but I didn't. My original excitement about living in Spain was obliterated by all my preconceived but unfulfilled notions about what life would be like, what I should be like, and by my inability to release myself from the past, from Mexico. I compared Spain to Mexico and complained about the differences. Afraid of unfamiliar things, I wanted my comfort zone back.

For more than two years in Spain I clung to wishes and memories. Then, during our final year, I began to focus on Spanish charm and to let go of my old comfort zone as I kept stumbling over surprising "ah-ha"experiences: "Ah-ha! This is a beautiful country!" "Ah-ha! This is fascinating history!" "Ah-ha! I love these people."

I was still "ah-ha-ing" in amazement, falling head over heels in love, even as we departed. Next long-term stop: Brazil—where all too soon I returned to old patterns, comparing Brazil to my most recent comfort zone, to Spain. I didn't know how to establish a new comfort zone, how to conquer my fear of the unfamiliar. I didn't accept my surroundings on their own merits. Because my mind was initially imprinted with negative data (differences), I didn't bother to look for things to love.

I continued to cultivate resentment until I caught a new mind-set through understanding mortality's realities and the joy of individuality, flexibility, and freedom. From these experiences, I learned to love the past, the present, and the future all at the same time and I promised to never again allow life, either the mundane or the exotic, to pass me by.

After almost fifteen years in Brazil, when the time finally came to move once more, we began to divest ourselves of accumulated possessions including a ranch of gorgeous 200-acre proportions. Some

111

people, thinking that after fifteen years as residents we would eventually return, asked why we would sell such a piece of paradise. The difficult answer was that, much like leaving my beloved Texas, in leaving my beloved Brazil I knew it would be a long time, if ever, before I would live there again. A friend who had forfeited her own piece of paradise to accept an international assignment, commented kindly about the ranch sale: "There is maturity in knowing when to let go." Though that may be true, it still isn't easy. Those who think it's easy to say goodbye have never had to say goodbye.

Saying goodbye to Brazil was not easy, but this time I had a new frame of mind and I had learned correct principles. From much practice I had learned how to hold on and how to let go. I kept the memories and the lessons. I had developed enough faith to deal with the unknown in a positive way. I let go of wishes for the same apartment, the same friends, the same grocery store, the same language, the same church calling, the same routine—things that could not and would not go with me. I didn't forget them. I just left them where they belonged: happy thoughts in my mind and heart. I could do that because I had learned to look at the needs of the circumstances, live in the spirit of the moment, abandon the itsy-bitsy contracts of personal preference and take a chance on involvement in something new and different.

I had learned that variety is good, that flexibility is freedom, that change is healthy. Exchanging an old comfort zone for a new one can be a very good thing.

We left Brazil one Monday morning with seven large suitcases and one small dog. By nightfall, we were settled in Santiago, Chile. The next morning, I began to trade Portuguese for some very rusty Spanish and to practice juggling new and different things. Though I had moments of nostalgia, no cloud of resentment materialized—and that remained true even a few months later when events in Chile left me alone and plunged me into a future of totally unexpected and unwanted unknowns. Even then, I felt free to face those unknowns with faith and hope.

Holding on to old things that don't work anymore is fraught with stress and structure. The only resolution to the problem is to think differently, change, adapt. We only hang onto old comfort zones because we don't know how to make new ones and feel squeamish about the uncertainty. Changing is an adventure that requires faith and hope to live with flexibility and individuality. We stay bound to non-essential habits and traditions because we sense some type of order there. We feel in control. Outside that zone there might be no obvious guidelines, precision, or specifications. There might even be confusion or chaos.

Outside our comfort zones we might need to think differently, rely on spontaneity, practice. Because of opposition, choice, and inexperience there can be a strong sense of risk and fear.

Some fears, those that keep us from danger, are good. Others are not so good as they keep us from overcoming our weaknesses and finding personal progress. They include concerns such as: "What if I get my feelings hurt?" "What if I can't do it?" "What if people don't approve?" "What if it's hard?" "What if I lose control?" "What if I make a mistake?" The words "what if" indicate risk. When we don't like the risk percentages, we hold on to the old at all costs. We seem not to realize that risk is everywhere. It's only a matter of which risks we choose to take. The same "what if's" exist in the old comfort zone but, because we're familiar with the territory, the risks seem smaller and more manageable. We would give ourselves more freedom and options, be less like the third servant in the parable of the talents, if we would just realize that risk is inseparably connected to living.

Everything about life is risky: bathtubs are slippery, food contains germs, acid-rain and cancer-sunshine fill the air, and the evening news is enough to force us off the streets permanently—but then there could be an earthquake, a flood, or a tornado and our house might collapse around us. We are surrounded by risky situations. We can constantly err on the side of caution, relegating ourselves to familiar territory, or we can give up a little precision and, with faith and hope, risk a little more, live a little more. Caution that keeps us from danger is good, but caution that binds us unremittingly to old comfort zones only plants seeds of stress and structure.

Every day we do a myriad number of things almost unconsciously because of a type of faith. We drive the car believing it will get us to our destination. We get on airplanes with faith in the mechanics and the pilots. We eat believing the food is safe. We send children to school believing they will be reasonably well taught. Whenever doubt and fear enter with any degree of intensity, action ceases, faith evaporates.

But if we could always remember our divine nature—that we are children of our Father in Heaven, and that we have within us sparks of His divine characteristics—we would never allow fear and doubt to win. We would let Him help us develop an abundance of faith and hope—of "mind power."

Mind power is having the ability to take charge of our own attitudes, behaviors, and feelings. Eleanor Roosevelt once said that no one can make us feel inferior without our permission. That is mind-power. No one, not even the devil, can make us do anything if we do not choose to do it. With mind power, we can focus on dark things or bright things. We can decide whether our "glass" is half-full or whether it is half-empty. Mind power controls body, emotions, attitudes, even spiritual well-being. Determination is produced in the mind. Instinct is regulated, controlled and trusted by a wise, focused mind. Experience is filed, sorted and integrated through mind power. Commitment, desire, and joy are born in the mind. Sacrifice is accepted in the mind. And they can all be snuffed out, eliminated, in that same all-powerful location. Fear and doubt or faith and hope win or lose in the mind.

There have been times when mind power, fortified by the Spirit, was all I had to go on: a difficult foreign assignment endured to the end when it would have been so easy to quit in the middle and go home; a stake calling of mammoth proportions made doubly difficult because I was weak in the language in which I needed to work; that university summer semester nearly abandoned more than once because I had to acquire prerequisite information for the courses on my own initiative simultaneously with a full-course load. Those were stretching experiences of one kind. Then I found I had to learn to use mind power to relax and to find gratitude and joy in the challenges and tragedies of life. I needed mind power to practice as well as to say "no" to temptation and to too many service projects. Mind power brings success, and it provides peace.

With faith and hope providing mind power to overcome fears, we can stay steady as we travel the rough road of life.

As Paul said: "For God hath not given us the spirit of fear; but of power, and of love, and of a sound mind" (2 Timothy 1:7). Paul used mind power to fulfill his mission. He concluded: "I have fought a good fight, I have finished my course, I have kept the faith....." (2 Timothy 4:7).

Success, peace, joy, assertiveness, compassion—whatever it is we need, we've got what it takes to get it: mind power and spiritual assistance. Because mortality is a place of opposition, choice, and inexperience, learning to use the power of our minds is a process. Because we have a divine heritage and divine guidance, we can succeed. And if we just unearth some honesty, we can sincerely articulate and challenge our fears.

When I began to cautiously change my frame of mind, I found a surprising fear. I had been a creature of programmed seriousness for so long that I didn't know if I would still be myself if I became more optimistic and enthusiastic. I didn't know what others might think of me. I wasn't sure what I would think of myself. Having an underlying "fear of fun," I prided myself on appearing solemn and "mature." I wondered if I would look childish and silly if I suddenly became spontaneous and enthusiastic.

The uncertainty was so pervasive that I posted a note by my desk that said: "You will not lose your identity by loosening up." And I didn't. In fact, the more I released myself from stress and structure, the more truly me I became and the more I liked the true me. I found out who I was supposed to be before society turned me into a carbon copy. Enjoying life may be childlike, but it is not childish; and in true enjoyment is true maturity. "Fun" does not have to be hedonistic or boisterous. It can be individualized and infused into life any time, any place to make any day more joyful and, sometimes, more bearable.

We recoil from abolishing our itsy-bitsy contracts because we think they define who we are and yet, in them, we are never really ourselves. In them we do things because we think it is what other people expect of us or will not criticize, or even what we unwittingly expect of ourselves.

We often fear what others might say or think, but when we learn about the power of taming the masquerade or letting go of the letter of the law, it is expedient for us to conquer the fear and, with faith, embrace the new, liberating principles.

If we fear making mistakes because of our weakness and inexperience, we will think it best to stay where we feel more secure. We hear mostly of people who successfully challenged their fears but, it is certain that in the process of succeeding, they had their hesitant steps into the unknown—even times when they failed and had to try again.

Much of the fear of leaving comfort zones has to do with fear of losing control. What if I can't keep everything and everyone under my thumb? What if the "pictures" I painted for the future don't come to be? What if the agenda I planned and prepared does not materialize? In truth, the plans we make very rarely come to pass in exactly the way we expect. We might as well accept that reality before the fact rather than after and, therefore, write all those plans in pencil with a very large eraser. An alternative title for life is "constant adjustment."

Like my fear of losing my identity, perhaps we all have some surprising fears such as fear of quiet time. We can be so connected to the treadmill of life, the quicksand, that we don't know what to do without it. If this is the case, our comfort zone is, no doubt, very uncomfortable and it will take some practice to create a new one—remembering that there is maturity in knowing when to let go. It is worth it to take the risk, to be still and quiet sometimes and sense the depth of life and love and options and self.

One of the most amazing facts is that once we are comfortable with mortality's inherent risks and realities, the less we think about fears and the more we move easily into the unknown. Usually we need faith before answers come. President Harold B. Lee said that sometimes it is necessary to take a step into the dark before the lights come on (*The Holy Temple;* Boyd K. Packer; Bookcraft, Inc.; Salt Lake City, Utah; 1980; 184.) With faith, we begin to understand that once we take that first step, the lights of understanding almost always come on and confidence clicks in.

Competition, comparison, and achievement create fear and make us pessimistic. In the quicksand, everything seems so impossible. If we insist on perfection, we will always be caught between the social need to appear precise and flawless and the imprecision of mortality's realities that demands faith and spontaneity. Faith requires that we abandon the fear of imperfection and be willing to risk and try and maybe fail, and try, try, again. Faith is a willingness to move forward, with courage, trusting God.

"If men were duly to consider themselves, and turn their thoughts and reflections to the operation of their own minds, they would readily discover that it is faith, and faith only, which is the moving cause of all action in them; that without it both mind and body would be in a state of inactivity, and all the exertions would cease, both physical and mental" (*Lectures on Faith* 1:10; compiled by N.B.Lundwall; Bookcraft, Inc.; Salt Lake City, Utah).

The apostle Peter learned in a remarkable way about the power of doubt and fear to halt action and extinguish faith.

After feeding the 5,000, Jesus went up into a mountain to pray. Then in the middle of the night, having concluded His meditation, He went to find His disciples who were on a ship in the middle of a storm-tossed Sea of Galilee. Jesus, hastening to reach them, chose the most direct route: walking across the water. His disciples, seeing Him, were afraid thinking he was a ghost or a spirit until He called to them and identified Himself. Peter, recognizing the exciting possibilities, said to Jesus: "Lord, if it be thou, bid me come unto thee on the water." Jesus had no objection to Peter's request and said to him simply: "Come."

Peter must have had to exert some physical effort to climb over the side of the rocking, bouncing ship, but his faith was sufficient. He maneuvered himself to the churning surface of the sea and began, with total confidence, to walk toward the Savior. Suddenly, however, the seeds of doubt sprouted. How could he do this? After all, water was water, the wind was raging, and he was a mere mortal! By feeling insecure in being outside his comfort zone and beyond the realm of normal mortal experience, faith flipped to fear and Peter began to sink. Suddenly terrified he cried out in panic, "Lord save me. And immediately Jesus stretched forth His hand, caught him, and said unto him, "Oh thou of little faith, wherefore didst thou doubt?" (Matt. 14:21-31).

How often does that same question apply to us? How often do we fear the uncertain nature of life, insecure with our own mortality? How often does that fear keep us from venturing out of our comfort zones? How often do we doubt?

On another occasion Jesus said that if we had faith only as large as the grain of a mustard seed, we could move mountains (Matt. 17:20). And He said: "Be not afraid, only believe" (Mark 5:36). Fear of adapting, changing, doing hard things doesn't come from the Lord. He has given us power, love, and a strong mind. We can face and conquer any dragons between us and the unknown allowing us to be able to fulfill any difficult short term or long term mission.

While it is true that the kind of fear that keeps us from danger is good, the fear that keeps us from applying gospel principles and exercising faith needs to be overcome. If we look at those in history who confidently went and did the Lord's bidding, we find faith, nothing wavering.

Abraham was told to take his son, Isaac, his only son whom he loved, and go into the land of Moriah and offer him there for a burnt offering. "And Abraham rose up early in the morning...and went unto the place of which God had told him" (Genesis 22:3).

When we read of this incredible event, we tend to ask "How?" How could Abraham willingly, unflinchingly do such a thing?

Part of the answer is in Hebrews 11:17-19: "By faith Abraham, when he was tried, offered up Isaac: and he that had received the promises offered up his only begotten son, of whom it was said, That in Isaac shall thy seed be called: Accounting that God was able to raise him up, even from the dead; from whence also he received him in a figure."

Abraham had no doubts in God or in the fulfillment of the promises. If miracles had to happen to bring those promises to pass, then he had complete confidence, complete faith, that miracles would happen. He would obey, nothing wavering, and leave the miracles to the Lord.

Likewise, Alma trusted enough to do hard things. He taught the people of Ammonihah but was rejected.

"Now when the people had said this, and withstood all his words, and reviled him, and spit upon him, and caused that he should be cast out of their city, he departed thence and took his journey towards the city which was called Aaron... behold an angel of the Lord appeared unto him saying... I am sent to command thee that thou return to the city of Ammonihah and preach again unto the people of the city... Now it came to pass that after Alma had received his message from the angel of the Lord he returned speedily to the land of Ammonihah..." (Alma 8:13-18).

Alma had no hesitation, in spite of the fact that the atmosphere in Ammonihah was hostile. He would act, based on faith, secure in his relationship with the Lord.

The Prophet Joseph Smith went to Carthage peacefully, in faith: "I am going like a lamb to the slaughter, but I am calm as a summer's morning; I have a conscience void of offense towards God, and towards all men. I shall die innocent, and it shall yet be said of me—he was murdered in cold blood" (Doc. & Cov. 135:4).

Esther of the Old Testament took a huge risk in going before the king to plead for the life of her people, the Jews in Babylon. The situation required it, and she was equal to the task. Nephi and Sam willingly went back to Jerusalem for the brass plates (Laman and Lemuel went "all bent out of shape," in a cloud of resentment) because the situation required it. The prophets Samuel and Nathan delivered messages of condemnation to kings they loved because it was necessary.

I like to believe that Eve took a long look at the context of her mission before eating the fruit of the tree of knowledge of good and evil. Afterwards Adam, too, made his choice based on good, common sense—although it entailed a huge, unknown equation filled with risk.

Do we ever stop to think of how difficult it must have been for these people to abandon their comfort zones? The trust and commitment, the conquest of doubt and fear, is so evident in the words and lives of these examples, our examples. To become like them, to handle life's tragedies and challenges, to conquer fear and face the unknown, we must develop similar trust and confidence in ourselves, our fellowmen, and our God. Though God never fails and never fails us, we may fail ourselves or each other. He knows this, yet He gives us agency and entrusts so much in our hands that we may gain experience and knowledge.

We need faith in God. We must know He exists and have a correct idea of His character, perfection, and attributes (*Lectures on Faith* 3:34;

compiled by N.B. Lundwall; Bookcraft, Inc.; Salt Lake City, Utah). When we understand that His power is manifest in love, that His work is to bring to pass our immortality and eternal life (Moses 1:39), and that He has no other motive, then we will have faith and confidence in Him, in His plans for us, and in His requests of us.

Today we often look to the Mormon pioneers in awe and wonder asking if we could have done what they did. The answer of course is "yes," if we had their faith—their frame of mind. Because of their unwavering confidence in their Father in Heaven, the Savior, the plan of salvation, and the counsel of their leaders they faced desert, disease, and death as they moved on from Nauvoo the beautiful to the desolate valley of the Great Salt Lake. Husbands accepted callings to serve missions in distant lands for indefinite periods of time, far from their families, without even telephones or a good mail system to keep in touch or fast jets to bring them quickly home. Wives and children tearfully but willingly kissed their husbands and fathers farewell, all because they had faith, trust, nothing doubting.

"But," we say, "I trust God, the Savior, my leaders, and the plan. Why do I feel so unsure, so insecure?" Perhaps we waver more than we should because in today's skeptical society, we so easily doubt ourselves. Just as Peter's attempt to walk on water was nullified because he doubted himself, his ability as a mortal to deal with the elements, so we doubt our own capabilities to deal with our environment. Walking on water is not our challenge but because society is critical, we have difficulty laying hold on sufficient trust to generate unwavering faith. Unlike Nephi who clearly stated that, in returning to seek Laban and acquire the brass plates, he was led by the Spirit not knowing before-hand what to do (1 Nephi 4:6), we can't go without a blueprint.

It is only with faith that we can handle the uncertainty and the spon-taneity of moving out and on with no map, no specific instructions. God has not given us the spirit of fear. With faith as our passport, we can pack our bags with confidence, optimism, and little mind power. We'll learn to rely on our internal compass as we leave our comfort zones and are led by the Spirit. One reason the letter of the law killeth is that it does not engender much faith.

"For behold, it is not meet that I should command in all things; for he that is compelled in all things, the same is a sloth-ful and not a wise servant; wherefore he receiveth no reward.

"Verily I say, men should be anxiously engaged in a good cause, and do many things of their own free will, and bring to pass much righteousness;

"For the power is in them, wherein they are agents unto themselves. And inasmuch as men do good they shall in no wise lose their reward.

"But he that doeth not anything until he is commanded, and receiveth a commandment with doubtful heart, and keepeth it with slothfulness, the same is damned" (Doc. & Cov. 58:26-29).

The power is in us! We are free to step into the unknown, to live by the spirit, to reject the masquerade, to practice and improve, to exercise faith—and the Lord doesn't leave us to work our spontaneity in a vacuum. He never has and never will. He has told us how to get help, His help:

"...Behold, I say unto you, that you must study it out in your mind; then you must ask me if it be right, and if it is right I will cause that your bosom shall burn within you; therefore, you shall feel that it is right. But if it be not right you shall have no such feelings (Doc. & Cov. 9:8-9).

He will instruct us, guide us, in our minds and in our hearts (Doc. & Cov. 8:2).

In reality, the risks and unknowns of mortality require that we learn to work by faith, to walk by faith. Much of the ability to do that is bound up in faith's close companion: hope.

Today's society is a nightmare of constant failure and falling short, of self-deprecation and other-deprecation. Nothing is ever good enough. No one is ever good enough. Experts say that all of us have moments of discouragement, but the difference between a pessimist and an optimist is that the optimist knows how to reverse the downward spiral and counter negatives with positives (see *Learned Optimism;* Martin E.P. Seligman, Ph.D.; Pocket Books; New York, N.Y.; 1990).

People who hold on to happiness, even in the midst of discouraging circumstances, possess that vital key of optimism: hope. They can see the light at the end of the tunnel. Hope pulls us to the light—although it often takes mind power and a big push from the Spirit.

The power of gospel hope was taught to me on a balmy December night in Brazil. I was back home after spending a couple of weeks in the United States dealing with some family problems and needs. I had jet lag and a host of conflicting thoughts. I didn't want to be confused and sad three days before Christmas, but it happened anyway. Though I was glad to be back, I found myself alone for the weekend trying to wade through a mountain of paperwork and lingering memories.

To escape, I turned on the television to a movie I had long intended to see. The film, however, was violent and depressing. I had some interest in seeing the end, the resolution, but I began changing channels while I waited, looking for a brighter side. Unfortunately, the other options seemed worse than the first, and I sensed the power of the adversary to over-run our lives with darkness if we allow him in.

Finally, I returned to the movie only to discover that there was no resolution in the finale. Instead, there were just more questions about the nature of evil and our ability to do battle. Feeling a kind of claustrophobia enfold me, I decided to go out for a walk. The night was warm and humid as I began strolling through the forty acres of our apartment complex, absorbing the beauty of the Christmas lights that shimmered in various types of scattered trees. I walked and thought and, after about thirty minutes, sat down on a white bench near the decorative waterfall at the entrance to the complex. Multi-colored holiday lights illuminated the cascading water and a twinkling star shone down from the top of the highest tree.

My thoughts turned to Christmas and then to music. Many songs and hymns have taken up residence in my heart and even changed my life but none of them, I mused, were Christmas carols. Perhaps some

Christmas melody could dispel the little black cloud that was obscuring my sunshine.

Quietly I hummed a couple of traditional favorites. They were tunes full of the spirit of the season and I was ever so grateful for their message, a message not eclipsed by the little black cloud. Christmas for me was both the peace of the manger and the glory of the resurrection, and my heart sang with joy even though a cloud of sadness drifted aimlessly through my mind.

And then I remembered that other song, the one we sing occasionally at Christmas time. I wasn't sure I knew all the words but, haltingly, I started to whisper them, sensing that somewhere in those lyrics there was a message for me.

I heard the bells on Christmas Day
Their old familiar carols play,
And wild and sweet the words repeat
Of peace on earth, good will to men.

The contradiction between the message of those "old familiar carols" and the darkness that had invaded my life was apparent. Peace on earth? Not if the enemy has his way.

I thought how, as the day had come,

The belfries of all Christendom

Had rolled along th' unbroken song

Of peace on earth, good will to men."

The unbroken song had been interrupted for me. I was acutely aware of the infiltration of evil into so much of society.

And in despair I bowed my head:

"There is no peace on earth," I said,

"For hate is strong and mocks the song

Of peace on earth, good will to men."

I understood the perspective of the poet. Hate *is* strong. Where *is* the peace? Nevertheless a prompting urged, "Sing on." I searched for the words to the next verse.

Then pealed the bells more loud and deep:

"God is not dead, nor doth he sleep;

The wrong shall fail, the right prevail,

With peace on earth, good will to men."

Those words, words of truth and hope, cascaded in like the bubbling waterfall before me, and the little black cloud fled in haste. Yes, evil would have its day but its death sentence had already been announced. Though it might win numerous battles, it would never win the war. Christmas, the birth and mission of the Savior of the world, had insured its ultimate and permanent defeat. Because of Jesus, peace and goodwill can reign in our hearts and in our little corner of the world even now, and eventually everywhere—forever.

I had been given a new frame of mind.

With sunshine restored, I soon reluctantly left the peaceful waterfall and the lights and the star; but I took the memory, the message, and the music.

Till ringing, singing, on its way,

The world revolved from night to day,

A voice, a chime, a chant sublime,

Of peace on earth, good will to men!

(*Hymns*, 214; italics added.)

That night I realized that hope can always be found in Christ. The works of darkness are frustrated in Him. Death is conquered because of

Him. Sin is overcome because of Him. Agency is available to us because of Him. We can be mortal, imperfect, and because of Him we can be made whole and return to our Father in Heaven. How grateful, how humble we should be to know that even our imperfect mortality does not nullify the possibilities.

We can have hope in many aspects of life, but it seems that without hope in Jesus Christ pessimism thrives—as does inequality, rigidity, prejudice, criticism, pride. Not too many years ago, science sent out the rumor, "God is Dead." At that moment, hope and optimism began to vanish. True hope is not in a laboratory or in a test tube. It is in the mission of the Savior of the world.

When faith and hope are practiced consistently, even though not perfectly, they yield the mind power necessary to challenge the dragons of fear, doubt, and discouragement. In faith and hope are the energy of the gospel, a willingness to live by the spirit, forfeit the masquerade, and practice within the realm of mortality's realities. The purpose in doing so is not to prove something about being courageous or untraditional. The purpose is simple and basic: to find true love—love for God, for self, for others.

With discouragement and fear, love shrinks. With faith and hope, love blossoms.

CHARITY:

FOR THE LOVE OF SQUARE PEGS AND PRODIGALS

"Remember, the worth of souls is great in the sight of God" (Doc.& Cov. 18:10).

Years ago, I cut a picture from a magazine and filed it in a folder titled "love." In the picture, a brown and white puppy with a forlorn look in its eyes is receiving a comforting lick on the cheek from a small cream-colored cat. Differences shouldn't keep us from caring for each other, but the kind of canine-feline affection in the photo is rare. Usually we fight like ordinary dogs and cats.

Because of the nature of mortality—because none of us are perfect, because we are all sinners in one way or another—we should maintain a humility and sensitivity that allows us to see the truth: we are all square pegs and prodigals in some form. We are all different shapes and sizes with different gifts and needs. There is no mold into which we can all be forced to fit (though Satan will try). And since the worth of souls is great in the sight of God, it behooves us to love rather than to judge. While there are some truly dangerous people around, they are a minority. Since each of us can qualify as a square peg or prodigal, we cannot go through life avoiding people who are simply different.

Jesus was criticized for mingling with publicans and sinners. His reply was "They that be whole need not a physician but they that are sick" (Matt. 9:12). Elder Glenn L. Pace of the Seventy has suggested that we cannot follow the Savior's injunction to be the salt of the earth if we "stay in one lump in the cultural halls of our beautiful meeting-houses" (*Ensign;* © Intellectual Reserve, Inc.; Nov. 1990; 8). We have a responsibility to reach out, in sincere friendship, and safely include diverse types of people. Even if we are as different as dogs and cats, we must esteem our brothers and sisters as ourselves, remembering that our diversity does not change the truth: We are all "sons and daughters, children of a king" (*Hymns*, 249). We are royalty. We so easily over-look this one grand similarity.

I have lived in many different cultures and environments, both domestically and internationally. Only in one did I feel that I was crit-icized and rejected, that I could never measure up to expectations. It was neither a pleasant nor an easy experience. Unfortunately, I can name many places where I was the one doing the criticizing and reject-ing. Self-righteousness is a weakness of mere mortals that must be con-quered and re-conquered. It originates, in many cases, in expectations of conformity—wanting everyone to be the same. The scriptures only ask for conformity in the state of our hearts, in our ability to follow the Master and love our fellowmen. To show love, we have to accept and embrace diversity.

Some years ago, I happened to visit two different wards on a day when the Relief Society lesson focused on diversity. The lesson in the first ward detoured from the manual and assimilated an attitude of humorous condescension about differences. By contrast, in the second ward the lesson conveyed the intended message of the joy of diversity. Sometime later I attended a testimony meeting in the second ward where I heard many from obviously diverse nationalities, economic means, and family status speak emotionally about feeling so at home in that ward. Reflecting on those Relief Society lessons, I understood why—and I wondered if any of those speakers would have felt so welcome in the first ward.

A friend of mine, a less active member, was visiting with member friends on a Sunday. She had a sudden impulse to accompany them to Sacrament meeting but was effectively discouraged because she was dressed in slacks. To my knowledge, she didn't ever feel an impulse to attend church again. Another similar story tells of a young farm boy who went to Sunday School for the first time in the only clothes he had: some tattered jeans and a threadbare shirt. After class, his teacher suggested he come the next time dressed more appropriately. There was no next time.

The Book of Mormon clearly teaches that all are welcome: "...he inviteth them all to come unto him and partake of his goodness; and he denieth none that come unto him, black and white, bond and free, male and female; and he remembereth the heathen; and all are alike unto God, both Jew and Gentile" (2 Nephi 26:33).

We are familiar with this verse and this concept, yet we are not so eager to invite everyone. We sometimes have trouble including people of different cultures and races and languages. We have a tendency to shy away from those who are, in any way, a little bit different. And the words "bond and free," interpreted for today, could mean that some of us are blessed to be free financially, free of physical challenges, free of visible bad habits, free of sin, free of phobias, free of the unique difficulties of being a minority. Some have truth, others are not so free. Nevertheless, all need to be invited and included. All of us learn and grow and change by belonging, by being appreciated and loved, not by being criticized.

Peter, as head of the Church in the meridian of time, needed to make a major change in Church perspective and policy regarding diversity. As a result, he was given a revelation wherein he "saw heaven opened, and a certain vessel descending unto him, as it had been a great sheet knit at the four corners, and let down to the earth: Wherein were all manner of fourfooted beasts of the earth, and wild beasts, and creeping things, and fowls of the air. And there came a voice to him, Rise, Peter: Kill, and eat. But Peter said, Not so, Lord; for I have never eaten anything that is common or unclean. And the voice spake unto him again the second time, What God hath cleansed, that call not thou common" (Acts 10:11-14).

This vision was given to teach Peter that, unlike prior times when only the Jews were the Lord's select flock and only the Jews were given the opportunity to receive the gospel, now the good news was to go to all mankind. The animals mingling together in the great sheet of the revelation were diverse species that were "unclean" or unacceptable, to be avoided at all costs under the law of Moses. Hence Peter's fearful response that he had never broken the law, never partaken of anything common or unclean. Then he is told to not be afraid for the rule is changed. God has cleansed those things that were once anathema. They are no longer to be avoided.

Circumstances immediately gave Peter an application to the symbolism in the dream. One Cornelius, who was not a Jew, desired to hear the gospel. Peter went to him, and declared: "Ye know how that it is an unlawful thing for a man that is a Jew to keep company, or come unto one of another nation; but God hath shewed me that I should not call any man common or unclean" (Acts 10:28). Following this event, the word was preached to all nations and peoples. The gospel net began to gather all kinds.

Prophets have told us to liken all scripture to our own circumstances for our profit and learning (1 Nephi 19:23). While, to Peter, this was a stunning revelation, with the worldwide missionary effort today we have no problem understanding that the gospel is to go to all nations and people. Instead, today we have a challenge dealing with the resulting mix of diversity. All the "fourfooted beasts and wild beasts and creeping things and fowls of the air" have to mingle together, and we must learn to "not call any man common or unclean." Just because we are "gathered" does not mean we will all be alike, and those who have not yet gathered will be even more different.

We must reach out to others and join in the purpose of building the kingdom, each with his or her own gifts, but without losing our identities. We will still be "beasts" and "creeping things" and "fowls." We will still be "dogs" and "cats." We will still be different races and nationalities, speak different languages. We will think differently, dress differently, wear our hair differently. We will learn differently, and we will help differently because we will come from different backgrounds and have different life experiences. As Paul indicated, the diversity is an asset (1 Cor. 12). In the diversity, we share and we learn and we grow. That is how it should be in the gospel for the gospel of Jesus Christ will always gather of all kinds, not just one kind; and, even within the gospel, we will retain our individuality. Enjoying the extensive diversity will allow us to embrace all the "beasts," "creeping things" and "fowls," to comfort all the "dogs and cats" in our corner of the world.

After the visit of Christ to the Americas as recorded in the Book of Mormon, the people developed a unique, peaceful society. It is often called the golden era of the Book of Mormon. We know that the people were all disciples of Jesus Christ and that there were no contentions and disputations among them, an attribute mentioned three times in the first fifteen verses of Fourth Nephi. That account also explains the reason for their camaraderie: "...because of the love of God which did dwell in the hearts of the people" (4 Nephi, vs. 15). There were no "Lamanites, nor any manner of -ites; but they were in one, the children of Christ, and heirs to the kingdom of God" (4 Nephi, vs. 17).

Contention is born of comparison, domination, pessimism, insecurity, prejudice and like attitudes, attitudes of the natural man who is always an enemy to God (Mosiah 3:19). The world would make "-ites" of all of us. The only way to overcome the tendencies of the natural man is to practice living a different lifestyle. For the Nephites of the golden era, there is indication that three years passed away before they could claim "no contentions and disputations among them" (4 Nephi, vs. 2). If each of us were to work diligently and pray sincerely each day for three years to eliminate negative characteristics from our lives we, too, might be able to claim no contention, no criticism, no prejudice, and much love.

In order to live the gospel, we need to embrace this lifestyle. It is the "Zion" attitude (Moses 7:18). Much of the problem in doing so is

142

that society, even the church society, does not live the gospel. In society appearance, achievement, and abilities are the criteria for worth; but in the gospel, those criteria have no value. "The worth of souls is great" has no qualifiers. Whether or not we have visible talents, prestigious awards, or photogenic physiques, does not matter. Neither does our behavior, our level of performance. Though blessings are predicated on obedience, we are all valuable and loved by our Father and His Son. Each mortal was and is worth the high and terrible price of the atonement. Although some of us may seem like strange creatures from outer space, we truly are all "sons and daughters, children of a king," each with his or her own special needs and own valuable gifts to contribute.

I found a representation of God's unconditional love in my experiences in Seville (Sevilla) Spain where my husband served as a mission president. Initially, my feelings for the area around me were less than loving.

Sevilla! How I hated it. That inhospitable, dilapidated, provincial, overgrown village in which I lived. In our various assignments around the world, I had coped with a lot of cities, but never anything quite like Sevilla. To me it seemed artificially arrogant in its lack of hospitality, and its provincialism existed by choice and tradition rather than as a natural result of location. Its crumbling old buildings simply looked unkempt instead of being sentinels of history and character, as old things often are.

And my feelings toward southern Spain, as a whole, were just as bleak.

In our travels, we went back and forth and up and down across the desolate landscape of southern Spain, the region called Andalucia. From the car window there was a monotonous view of olive trees, dead and dying sunflowers, and nothing. Miles and miles of nothing. Even the villages were repetitious, each one a duplicate of the last: small white-walled, red-roofed houses and shops surrounding a giant church steeple, all clustered at the base of a hill topped by a crumbling castle. Each village and castle served as a reminder that even though the knights and kings of old are gone, Spain does not quite exist in the present. Being a history buff, I was intrigued. I concluded, however, that I preferred studying history to living in it.

Then one balmy summer night, my negative feelings about Spain were altered forever.

We had been on a zone conference trip to the eastern side of the mission and were arriving back in Sevilla very late, just past midnight. As we crossed the railroad bridge and turned onto the tree-lined boulevard that rims the old city, my drowsiness was dispelled by a dazzling vista, the likes of which I had never seen.

A muted, golden glow from the radiance of hundreds of elegant, old-fashioned street lamps illuminated the city. Horse-drawn carriages, always available for hire by sight-seeing tourists, clippity-clopped up and down the street—and they had the lanes of the boulevard to themselves. There were few cars moving for the whole world was walking. Fathers and mothers sauntered along pushing babies in strollers. Children chased each other through parks. Young lovers cuddled on park benches. Teenage groups chatted and giggled on street corners. In the summer, Sevilla is only cool when the sun goes down. Everyone, it seemed, was out celebrating the night.

The golden glow intensified around the University where the ornate lamps stood closer together; and a block further on, spectacular lighting from Sevilla's immense cathedral beamed into the sky.

Astonished, I wondered where this Sevilla had been hiding for so long. As we drove away from the city center, I looked back at the glow feeling slightly giddy. I knew I was in love.

It was springtime when Andalucia came courting. The rains had soaked deep that year leaving the once brown landscape alive with velvet green crops and fields. Trees and bushes were thriving. The scent of cherry and orange blossoms hung heavy in the air. Those red and white country villages seemed to be captured on canvas and, in every direction, millions of multi-colored wild flowers bobbed and danced in the breeze.

The scene, serene but glorious, took my breath and ran with it. Only briefly did I bemoan how long it had taken me to embrace this country as I fell in love again.

And after that, again and again and again; with Cadiz and Cordoba, Granada and Almeria, with seacoasts and castles and mosques and mountains. But my first love was Sevilla: its Roman ruins, Moorish castle, Spanish cathedral.

I fell in love with Sevilla's Spring Fair, that late April festival when men, women and children don flamenco attire and with a "let's stop the world and have a party" attitude spend eight days and nights dancing at the fairgrounds.

I even fell in love with Holy Week, that peculiar pre-Easter spectacle so basically offensive to my testimony of the truth; yet so Spanish in its tradition and elegance. Years later when I thought of Sevilla, I would often imagine myself standing in the lamplight of the cathedral plaza watching those solemn processions: the hooded, long-robed men; penitents dragging their chains; and floats—huge gold-encrusted, fresh-flower-laden art exhibits topped by life-size statues, sometimes of the Virgin Mary, others depicting events in the last week of Jesus's life, and each propelled by seventy concealed and sweating men.

Because of Holy Week I better understood the traditions, the social pressures, that locked Spain and so many of its people in a prison of the past. Another short generation, I hoped, then the lock would be broken, then the people would seek the truth, then the Church in Spain would blossom as the rose. This I fervently hoped; for when I came to love the place, I found I loved its people, too.

These feelings became firmly rooted during our last ten months in Spain when my daughter, then three years of age, attended a small English pre-school located in the ancient alleys of Barrio de Santa Cruz—old town—around the cathedral. During the three hours each morning when she was three, I often roamed the narrow cobblestone streets, poked into tiny old shops, or just sat reading or meditating in the shade of quiet plazas. There I soaked up the sights, sounds, and smells of Sevilla. And there I realized I was no longer affected by the provincial attitudes and crumbling walls I had once hated so. Somewhere on the damp winding walkways of the old city, I had found the heart of Spain and its jewel, Sevilla. I had come to know something of its hidden beauty and, as a result, I loved it unconditionally.

"...the Lord seeth not as man seeth; for man looketh on the outward appearance, but the Lord looketh on the heart" (1 Samuel 16:7).

In Sevilla, I had a tiny taste of His kind of love. He sees past our crumbling walls and personal weaknesses. He knows our golden glow, our spring flowers. And we, too, can love a little bit as He does by taking time to find and understand the hidden beauties in those around us, beauties that are so often buried deep inside another's heart.

"The worth of souls is great in the sight of God." The worth of *every* soul is *always* great in the sight of God. His love has nothing to do with performance, appearance, status, *or even righteousness.* The principles of the plan allow Him to work for immortality and eternal life for all. No matter our station in life, we are divinely endowed and, because He looks on the heart, He loves us unconditionally. We have a responsibility to learn to love as He does.

Love thy neighbor as thyself (Luke 10:27). This commandment on love assumes that we love ourselves before we love our neighbor because, without vision of our self-worth through accepting our uniqueness and diversity including our weaknesses, we will inevitably be intolerant of uniqueness, diversity, and weakness in others. We will try to give everyone precisely our weight and dimension. But, in reverse, when we love ourselves and accept the "real us,"we will accept the "real them." Then we will see heart to heart and know, without doubt, that the worth of diverse souls is definitely very great.

As human beings, children of God, we always need to learn and improve while accepting and developing our uniqueness. Society's methods of directing everyone to march in time seem neat and tidy, at least on paper, but the truth is in the gospel. Diversity is a little unruly and requires more patience, but we can learn to hug the "dogs and cats" and even more unusual creatures around us. That's the only way to salt the earth a little bit with love.

Love is a ladder. We learn a little on each rung as we climb toward understanding and incorporating the ultimate love, Christlike love, that love called charity.

We rarely note that Paul's great discourse on diversity leads directly into his famous, humbling discussion of charity. Of the importance of diverse people and their diverse gifts Paul says: "But covet earnestly the best gifts: and yet shew I unto you a more excellent way" (1 Cor. 12:31). That more excellent way is charity.

"Though I speak with the tongues of men and of angels, and have not charity, I am become as sounding brass, or a tinkling cymbal.

"And though I have the gift of prophecy, and understand all mysteries, and all knowledge; and though I have all faith, so that I could remove mountains, and have not charity, I am nothing.

"And though I bestow all my goods to feed the poor, and though I give my body to be burned, and have not charity, it profiteth me nothing" (1 Cor. 13:1-3).

No gift, no talent, no service in and of itself, Paul says, can begin to compare with the value of charity. So that his listeners and readers might not assume that taking casseroles to the sick and afflicted is the sum total of charity, Paul elaborates:

"Charity suffereth long, and is kind; charity envieth not; charity vaunteth not itself, is not puffed up,

"Doth not behave itself unseemly, seeketh not her own, is not easily provoked, thinketh no evil;

"Rejoiceth not in iniquity, but rejoiceth in the truth;

"Beareth all things, believeth all things, hopeth all things, endureth all things.

"Charity never faileth...

"And now abideth faith, hope, charity, these three; but the greatest of these is charity" (1 Cor. 13:4-8, 13).

In the Book of Mormon, we learn why charity is counted as the greatest of the gifts.

"Wherefore, cleave unto charity, which is the greatest of all, for all things must fail—but charity is the pure love of Christ, and it endureth forever; and whoso is found possessed of it at the last day, it shall be well with him" (Moroni 7:46-47).

In Ether, Moroni further explains:

"...I remember that thou hast said that thou hast loved the world, even unto the laying down of thy life for the world, that thou mightest take it again to prepare a place for the children of men. And now I know that this love which thou hast had for the children of men is charity; wherefore, except men shall have charity they cannot inherit that place which thou hast prepared in the mansions of thy Father" (Ether 12:33-34).

We must have charity, the pure love of Christ, flowing from Him to us—and we always do. We must also have some of the same type of pure love flowing from us to others. We must seek and begin to acquire the kind of love He has—line upon line, precept upon precept, one step at a time. A love that never faileth.

In charity we find the spirit of the law, compassion, rather than the letter of the law, compulsion.

Charity suffereth long. Charity is not force, judgments, demands, and criticism. It is patience, teaching, and careful persuasion.

Charity is kind. Charity is not insistence on competition and achievement. It is negotiation, compromise, acceptance of individuality.

Charity envieth not. Charity does not require conformity, does not seek to climb the ladder of hierarchy. Charity is being yourself, peacefully, happily while still striving to improve in your time and way—and allowing others the same privilege.

Charity is not puffed up. It has no pride or desire to impress. It is quiet and caring.

Charity seeketh not her own. Charity is sincere. It seeks not to conquer and dominate. It does not overprotect or possess. It does not even covet what it has, rather it gives anything necessary if asked by the Lord.

Charity is not easily provoked. It is a soft answer and a sense of humor. Charity allows time and, therefore, requires patience.

Charity thinketh no evil. With charity, we will look for the good, minimize the bad, and optimistically hope for improvement.

Charity rejoiceth in truth. It is not controlled by skepticism or pessimism. It is happy and in search of truth wherever it might be found. It is an open mind, accepting and loving.

Charity believeth, beareth, hopeth, and endureth all things. Charity is fluid and selfless. It adapts easily based in the exercise of common sense. It is faith and trust, hope and optimism. It is respect for children of God and their diversity. It is seeking after that which is virtuous, lovely, or of good report and in doing good to all, not just to some. It is in choosing flexibility so we can value the right person, in the right way, at the right time.

With a focus on skepticism, pessimism, and criticism we will be mired in the stress of society and will find ourselves tense, critical, and grouchy; but with faith, hope, and charity—though we might be busily engaged—we will find our hearts brim full of peace. We are free to choose.

There is a famine of true love in the land, true love based on faith and hope—that love that is long suffering and kind, that pure love called charity. Charity never fails because it has no ulterior motive. It is pure love, nothing more.

"Perhaps the greatest charity comes when we are kind to each other, when we don't judge or categorize someone else. When we sincerely give each other the benefit of the doubt or remain quiet. Charity is accepting someone who has let us down; or resisting the impulse to become offended when someone doesn't handle something the way we might have hoped. Charity is refusing to take advantage of another's weakness, and being willing to forgive someone who has hurt us. Charity is expecting the best of each other" ("The Tongue Can be a Sharp Sword;" Marvin J. Ashton; *Ensign;* © Intellectual Reserve, Inc.; May 1992; 18).

Learning to love is a process, a process that is part of *becoming*, a process that is strong on feelings. From my experiences around the world and in my own neighborhood, I have learned that the feelings of love often leave us with surprise and with awe and wonder.

I had no idea I had so much to learn about love, but the metamorphosis began on that beautiful day in May when I was living in Brazil and Ayrton Senna, the nation's reigning national hero, died. He was their hero, in large measure, because he had loved them unconditionally. For three dark days, Brazilians mourned their loss. But then, on the fourth day, they made the sun to shine as they celebrated his life and gave their love to him in return for all he had given them.

Before that day, I had great difficulty loving people who were different. I wanted a robotic world of persons who all marched to the same drummer. And the Brazilians definitely had their own drummer—one who played samba music, even in troubled times, as the Brazilians danced. My drummer, on the other hand, played dirges, even in the best of times. At least that was the case until that day in May. On that day, I began to trade pessimism for optimism as the Brazilian people I had previously devalued taught me how to let the sun shine in. In consequence, I fell in love with an entire nation. In that love, I discovered new beauty and joy.

Nevertheless, I still had much to learn of love; some of which would be taught during one remarkable week in April.

I was in Salt Lake City one April evening with tickets to see the new film, *The Testaments*, at the Joseph Smith Memorial Building. I was awed by the power of the film and the story, a story of Christ's ministry in both the Old World and the New.

As I watched the numerous scenes depicting His love and His service, I was captivated by the joy that shone round about Him. My heart seemed to understand how much He loved people, how much He loved *me*, notwithstanding my weaknesses. I sensed the gentle majesty of His charity; and, though He was a man of sorrows (Mosiah 14:3, Isaiah 53:3), I knew that in His life there had been an abundance of joy. Emotions spilled over when I realized that if I was ever to be like Him, I would have to develop that same love and service and joy.

A day or two later, in the quiet reverence of the temple, wonder engulfed me in a ripple effect from the film. For the first time I recognized the very personal nature of the atonement. Yes, He died for all mankind. But, more, He died for *me*. I understood that, in some unfathomable way, His atonement was a very individual and personal event. "He *knows* me," my heart cried out—and not just me, but each one of us, no matter who we are; where we live, how we act. It is in this way that the atonement benefits *all* mankind, not in some generic sense, but because no one, *no one*, is exempt from His understanding and His love. And so, because He knows us by name and prays for each of us to come unto Him, He is a very personal Savior. The wonder of it enfolded me in the love of my Friend.

A few days later, leaving the parking garage of a downtown mall, I noticed a disheveled man and his worn and weary canine companion near the exit. "Homeless" read the sign he carried. Because I regularly give to organized charities, I rarely proffer donations to those on the street. In this moment, however, I felt compelled to find an offering. Frantically, my right hand reached for my wallet and fumbled for a bill. Five dollars was the lowest denomination available. Quickly I rolled down the window and motioned the man to come near. As he scanned the gift and whispered a choked thank you, tears welled up in his eyes and in mine. Though my vision blurred, I glanced in my side view mirror as I turned into the street and saw him stoop low to hug his dog. In that instant, a surge of joy took my breath away and I knew that, at times, I need to touch the hands and look into the eyes of those in need. It is a dawning of humility.

As that week ended, I sat with a friend who was suffering the consequences of tragic events and her own poor judgment. I reached out to her, to embrace her, not knowing what to say— and the Spirit spoke clearly: "It's okay." Confused, I flung the

words back as a question: "It's okay? How can this be okay?"
Then a calm settled over me as a distinct impression came:
"Just love her." And then I knew that she would learn and grow
from her experience—and so would I if I could simply love her.
Then everything would truly be okay.

I would not soon forget that April because it led directly into
May when new responsibilities required my constant interaction with a prodigal. Because I was at odds with some of his
behaviors, I prayed for distance, for a change, for an end to the
intrusion. But instead of comforting confirmation, a distinct
command invaded my being: "Learn to love him."

"What!?" I wailed. "Do *what?*" And I proceeded to question
the source, criticize the advice, rail against the truth—until I
lost the war and prayed, in tears, "Please, *please*, teach me
how."

And as our association continued, my eyes were opened bit
by bit. I began to see his gifts. I learned to value his clarity, his
sentimentality, his willingness to accept me. With a mellowing
of my heart, I found his—and I treasured his worth as a beloved
child of God.

The words of a song came to mind:

There are refugees among us

They don't carry flags or signs

They are standing right beside us

In the market checkout lines

And the war that they are fighting

It will not be televised

But the story of their need for love

Is written in their eyes.

(*Safe Harbors;* Michael McLean; Deseret Book Co.; Salt Lake City, Ut.; 1999).

He was a refugee—and so was I.

Years pass, and I continue to learn—albeit slowly. Perhaps my biggest hurdle was in deciding to let family members be themselves.

Love is a feeling—a wonderful feeling, but charity is more. Charity is acting on those feelings. The heart of charity is compassion, caring, and unconditional love. The father of the prodigal son had charity. He didn't berate his son for the wasted time and reckless behavior. He welcomed him home with compassion, caring, and unconditional love. The good Samaritan had charity. He provided all needful things for a stranger with compassion, caring, and unconditional love. Lehi felt charity for his sons, even rebellious Laman and Lemuel. Mormon felt charity for his people though they were about to destroy themselves in their iniquity. Charity often includes necessary counsel and correction, showing forth after an increase of love (Doc. & Cov. 121:43). From their hearts, Lehi and Mormon tried to make a difference in the lives of people who did not want to listen. They counseled, corrected, and always expressed their compassion, caring, and unconditional love.

When we practice charity we learn to provide patience, long suffering, and kindness. We give up perfectionism and give ourselves time to learn, opportunities to improve. We eliminate the brow-beating, the self-deprecation. We let ourselves be who we really are. And then we give others the same opportunity.

And charity is service. It is giving a party for the returning prodigal. It is paying at the inn for the wounded traveler by the roadside. It is taking time to teach, even teach those who really don't want to listen, in their time and in their way. Charity can be cakes and casseroles, volunteer work and priesthood blessings when those actions are filled with compassion, caring, and unconditional love. If they have no such qualities, there is no charity in them. Though helpful, they are just service projects, nothing more.

Service projects usually thrive outside the walls of our own homes, whereas charity, or the greatest need of it, often lives most completely inside. Charity's long suffering kindness is what makes a house a home. Without charity, a house is often just a hollow box full of demands, criticism, and unrealistic social expectations.

When we put charity into the context of mortality—giving ourselves and others merciful opportunities to learn, to grow, to change—we have a reason to always shout for joy. The mercy inherent in charity insures that charity never faileth.

MERCY:

WORTH SHOUTING ABOUT

"O give thanks unto the Lord; for he is good: because his mercy endureth for ever" (Psalms 118:1).

I love Victor Hugo's story, *Les Miserables*. I love the intensity, the opposition, the romance and, in the stage production, I love the music: *Bring Him Home* and *A Little Fall of Rain*. But it is the song *Stars* that helped me understand mortality's realities.

The story, which takes place during revolutionary days in France, has as its principle protagonists a policeman, Javert, and a former prisoner, Jean Valjean. In the story Jean Valjean, as a young man, steals a loaf of bread to feed his sister's starving family. He is captured by

Javert and summarily sentenced to years at hard labor. After serving the majority of his time, he manages to escape and, after receiving kindness and mercy from a parish priest, accepts the importance of repentance, changes his identity, devotes his life to good works, and becomes a wealthy and compassionate citizen. Javert, however, never stops hunting for him. Javert does not believe in repentance. He does not believe a "criminal" can change. He believes that justice must triumph. Anyone who makes a mistake must suffer forever. Therefore, Javert believes that he, himself, must never make a mistake. In the song *Stars*, Javert indicates that all things are fixed in their course, like the stars, and that this order is vital and cannot be changed.

Later in the story, when Jean Valjean has an opportunity to kill Javert and free himself from the constant hunt, he instead allows Javert to go free. To Javert, this is irreconcilable. In his universe, order is maintained by giving eternal punishment to all the imperfect who can never change. He cannot reconcile his concept of "once a criminal always a criminal" with Valjean's behavior. This confusing situation for Javert is compounded by the fact that, in his inflexible judgment, he, Javert, seems to have made a terrible mistake—a mistake that, by his own belief system, has condemned him to imperfection and eternal justice. He has erred and, therefore, cannot earn a heavenly reward. In this state of mental chaos, Javert chooses to end his life.

Javert and Jean Valjean are mirror images: one of justice, the other of mercy; one of punishment, the other of compassion; one of criticism and hopelessness, the other of faith and love.

Too often in our quest to be more perfect, more precise than mortality will allow, we become like Javert: living by the letter and the masquerade, with judgments and criticism, fearing justice for ourselves and demanding justice for others.

Though God is a just God, His plan is called the plan of mercy, the great plan of happiness. It is not the plan of justice or retribution.

Justice: fair, impartial, equal.

Mercy: leniency, compassion, forgiveness.

In the Book of Mormon, Alma speaks clearly of justice, mercy, and mortality's realities.

"And thus we see that all mankind were fallen, and they were in the grasp of justice; yea, the justice of God, which consigned them forever to be cut off from his presence."

And again, "there was no means to reclaim men from this fallen state, which man had brought upon himself because of his own disobedience" (Alma 42:14, 12).

The "justice of God" means that, though he loves us, he must be impartial; and since we are all imperfect because of the opposition, choice, and inexperience of mortality, we must all receive the punishment for imperfection.

But, Alma continues, the plan of mercy was brought about "to appease the demands of justice, that God might be a perfect, just God, and a merciful God also" (Alma 42:15). So, though God must meet the demands of the law, and they cannot be minimized or eradicated, there is a merciful way to appease those demands.

"And now, the plan of mercy could not be brought about except an atonement should be made, therefore God himself atoneth for the sins of the world, to bring about the plan of mercy, to appease the demands of justice..." (Alma 42:15).

Through the plan of mercy, Jesus would solve the problem for us.

The way these concepts work together is, to us and for us, a miracle: that Jesus could take upon Himself the pain and consequences of mortality and of sin, freeing us from having to endure the suffering demanded by the law of justice; and then, through our allegiance and repentance, grant us the kindness and compassion of mercy—in spite of the fact that we are still imperfect and undeserving.

"Listen to him who is the advocate with the Father, who is pleading your cause before him—

"Saying: Father, behold the sufferings and death of him who did no sin, in whom thou wast well pleased; behold the blood of thy Son which was shed, the blood of him whom thou gavest that thyself might be glorified;

"Wherefore, Father, spare these my brethren that believe on my name, that they may come unto me and have everlasting life (Doc. & Cov. 45:3-5).

Without an antidote to the strict law of justice there would be no route back, no way to repair damage done. Under Javert's type of doctrine, we would all be condemned unless we could live in perfect order and harmony like the stars. Too many of us believe like Javert: that we must do it all and do it all ourselves. Only then can Jesus save us. If that were true, why in the world did we all shout for joy?

The answer, of course, is that this is not true. Because of the fall, we are all imperfect. Through the Savior and His atonement, we can escape Satan's grasp and be granted glory.

This is mercy because we do not really deserve such kindness, compassion, and forgiveness. We are unworthy children. But our Father in Heaven, in His love, proposed the plan of mercy for all of us square pegs and prodigals. Our Savior, in His love, offered to provide the means, the atonement, that would put the plan of mercy into effect.

How great, how glorious, how complete,

Redemption's grand design,

Where justice, love and mercy meet

In harmony divine.

(*Hymns*, 195).

As I have tried to gain an understanding of the ways that the plan of mercy works for us, I have felt that mercy is a huge umbrella that reaches back to the pre-mortal existence and also covers us on earth, in the spirit world, and in eternity. The work of the gospel is to persuade everyone to accept the plan of mercy.

In pre-mortal life, the focus of the persuasive effort, the "missionary" effort, must have been to try and convince each one to accept our Father in Heaven's complete plan of mercy. Those who accepted the plan also accepted the imperfect conditions of mortality. This persuasion—by long suffering, gentleness, meekness, and love unfeigned (Doc. & Cov. 121:41)—must have been a challenge as many of the hosts of heaven decided to oppose it (Abraham 3:28; Rev. 12:9).

Those who rejected the plan did not want to participate in it and so their rebellion decreed that they be excluded, cast out from the presence of the Maker of the plan and all who followed Him. Their actions were a kind of mutiny since their objective, from the beginning, was to destroy the Father's plan of agency and put Satan's plan of force in its place. They received justice because they refused to accept the plan of mercy. Their plan was one of compulsion not compassion. Like Javert, they wanted a precise and perfect world (Moses 4:1-4).

Under the plan of mercy, our mortal foibles, large and small, are covered by the atonement. We are allowed time to learn and improve, and to learn and repent. Additionally, the atonement provides all the blessings of the gospel such as the sealing power, doctrinal clarity, spiritual guidance, and comfort in times of mortal trial. Then, the plan continues into the spirit world.

When we die, those who have already embraced the plan of mercy on earth continue to teach those who have not yet been persuaded, *even those who have heard it all before*:

"I beheld that the faithful elders of this dispensation, when they depart from mortal life, continue their labors in the preaching of the gospel of repentance and redemption, through the sacrifice of the Only Begotten Son of God, among those who are in darkness and under the bondage of sin in the great world of the spirits of the dead.

"The dead who repent will be redeemed, through obedience to the ordinances of the house of God,

"And after they have paid the penalty of their transgressions, and are washed clean, shall receive a reward according to their works, for they are heirs of salvation" (Doc. & Cov. 138:57-59).

Those in sin are usually identified as those who have willfully disobeyed. They knew the truth but chose not to follow. Nevertheless, they are taught, and through the ordinances of the temple, are redeemed and rewarded according to their works. Works, in this context, refers to their faith, repentance, acceptance of the ordinances and covenants of the gospel—their mighty change of heart.

This principle is emphasized in the parable of the prodigal son (Luke 15:10-32).

"Likewise," the story begins, "I say unto you, there is joy in the presence of the angels of God over one sinner that repenteth."

A man had two sons. The younger son chose to take his "goods," leave home, and spend everything in "riotous living." When his resources were gone, he found himself a servant feeding the swine of his master.

Humbled by his circumstances, he repented of his behavior and decided to return home and volunteer to be a servant to his father. As he approached his father's house, his father saw him coming. The son begged forgiveness and the father responded with fine apparel and a welcome home party, which angered the always obedient older son. He complained that he had been faithful "lo, these many years," but had never been treated with such honor.

The father, understanding mercy, replied "Son, thou art ever with me, and all that I have is thine. It was meet that we should make merry,

171

and be glad: for this thy brother was dead, and is alive again; and was lost, and is found."

The father in the story represents our Father in Heaven who, in His mercy and forgiveness, welcomes home every returning prodigal. All those who have been long faithful should stand with Him to "make merry and be glad." Along with the angels, we should all have joy over every "sinner that repenteth."

Because this story parallels the love of our Father in Heaven, the always faithful elder son would receive all the Father has, but so would the truly repentant younger son. The inheritance in eternity is not divided up among the heirs. Everyone who is worthy receives all.

We often suggest that it will be harder after this life to accept the gospel. Perhaps this will be so because we have built some walls with truth, through misconceptions and behavior, that we will take with us to the other side. But it is also true that some other walls, such as questions about life after death, should disappear once we have made that journey. Whether or not acceptance is more difficult beyond the veil than here on earth probably depends on the individual; but, even so, the way back may be more complex. "After they have paid the penalty of their transgressions" may signify a more difficult, more painful repentance process than that available in mortality. The important reality, however, is that the process of repentance and forgiveness is still in force.

Elder Orson F. Whitney cited words of the Prophet Joseph Smith:

"Though some of the sheep may wander, the eye of the Shepherd is upon them and sooner or later they will feel the tentacles of Divine Providence reaching out after them and drawing them back to the fold. Either in this life or the life to come, they will return. They will have to pay their debt to justice, they will suffer for their sins and may tread a thorny path; but if it leads them at last, like the penitent prodigal, to a loving and forgiving father's heart and home, the painful experience will not have been in vain. Pray for your careless and disobedient children. Hold on to them with your faith. Hope on, trust on till you see the salvation of God" (Orson F. Whitney, Conference Report, Apr. 1929, 110).

As we do all we can to reach out to others, especially to our family members, it is important to have faith and hope in the promises of the gospel.

"If you succeed in passing through these trials and afflictions and receive a resurrection, you will by the Power of the Priesthood, work and labor, as the Son of God has, until you get all your sons and daughters in the path of exaltation and glory. Therefore, mourn not because all your sons and daughters do not follow in the path that you have marked out to them or give heed to your counsels. Inasmuch as we succeed in securing eternal glory and stand as saviors, and as kings and priests to our God, we will save our posterity" (Lorenzo Snow; *Collected Discourses;* comp. Brian H. Stuy; 5 vols.; [1987-92], 3:364).

In contrast to these comforting teachings, we often refer to 2 Nephi 28:8-9 as an illustration that it is vain and foolish to think that any person choosing to live in selfish, uncharitable ways will ever be able to be saved:

"And there shall also be many which shall say: Eat, drink, and be merry; nevertheless, fear God—he will justify in committing a little sin; yea, lie a little, take the advantage of one because of his words, dig a pit for thy neighbor; there is no harm in this; and do all these things, for tomorrow we die; and if it so be that we are guilty, God will beat us with a few stripes, and at last we shall be saved in the kingdom of God. Yea, and there shall be many which shall teach after this manner, false and vain and foolish doctrines...."

The false and foolish doctrine in this verse is the suggestion that unchristlike behaviors can be justified and eternal rewards can be received without a change of heart, without repentance. With just a few stripes, all will be well. But forgiveness is only granted as a result of a change of heart and the resulting change of behavior on the part of each person. If a person's heart is changed, salvation, exaltation is at hand. Without a change of heart, this is not possible.

Mercy is also the principle taught in the parable of the laborers (Matt. 20:1-16). In this parable, a householder hires laborers to work in his vineyard. He hires some in the first hour of the day and some in the last hour. When the day ends, all the laborers receive exactly the same wage. Those who were hired early in the day murmur because they worked longer, bore more of the burden and, therefore, feel that they should receive more pay. But the goodman of the house replies: "Friend, I do thee no wrong: didst thou not agree with me for a penny?

Take that thine is, and go thy way: I will give unto this last, even as unto thee."

So it is under the plan of mercy. Those who have a change of heart, if it is truly a change of heart, even in the last hour, will be granted an inheritance in eternity equal to those who had a change of heart earlier on the time line. Only God knows our hearts, so only He can determine what is required, who qualifies, and when.

Those of us who are like the laborers of the first hour and are uncomfortable with the fact that the laborers who arrive in the last hour receive the same reward, should seek to embrace a little more of the plan of mercy.

The plan of mercy stretches its arms to bring in anyone, anytime. Let us not limit the plan of mercy in any way on anyone as that would put us in the position of judging improperly. Elder Dallin H. Oaks has said that, though we make judgments every day regarding choices in life, we should never presuppose the final judgment of anyone ("'Judge Not' and Judging;" *Ensign;* © Intellectual Reserve, Inc.; August 1999; 7).

To accept our need for mercy and to grant mercy to others is a humbling process. Mercy and humility are inseparably connected. They are the antithesis of pride. Pride is not new, but it has probably never before been so plentiful.

We live daily with a world order based on pride, a society full of people obsessed with doing it all themselves and proving that they are the best and the brightest, the most and the mightiest. Pride tells us to conform, compete, and achieve. Therefore, it is critical and judgmental, not compassionate, and when we buy into it we become uncompassionate people who cannot give mercy to ourselves and others.

President Ezra Taft Benson taught that enmity (hatred, hostility, a state of opposition) towards our fellowmen is a major cause of pride.

"Another major portion of this very prevalent sin of pride is enmity toward our fellowmen. We are tempted daily to elevate ourselves above others and diminish them.

"The proud make every man their adversary by pitting their intellects, opinions, works, wealth, talents, or any other worldly measuring device against others. In the words of C.S. Lewis: 'Pride gets no pleasure out of having something, only out of having more of it than the next man... It is the comparison that makes you proud: the pleasure of being above the rest. Once the element of competition has gone, pride has gone...'

"God will have a humble people. Either we can choose to be humble or we can be compelled to be humble. Alma said, 'Blessed are they who humble themselves without being compelled to be humble' (Alma 32:16).

"Let us choose to be humble. We can choose to humble ourselves by conquering enmity toward our brothers and sisters, esteeming them as ourselves, and lifting them as high or higher than we are" ("Beware of Pride;" *Ensign;* © Intellectual Reserve, Inc.; May 1989; 46).

Of the proud who cultivate enmity and the meek who shun it, Elder Neal A. Maxwell has observed:

"Meek individuals know they are set apart to serve, not merely set apart to observe. It is the proud, not the meek, who keep score. The meek are not playing games for those in the grandstand.

"The meek are slow to judge, whereas the proud are quick, even eager to judge. The meek will not withhold compassion or help, saying that 'the man has brought upon himself his misery' (Mosiah 4:17). Even though the individual may have done just that, they are nevertheless slow to judge. Being more open to the truth, the meek are more free, while the proud are compassed about with glitzed self-sufficiency that keeps them from grasping the hand of fellowship..." (*Meek and Lowly*; Neal A. Maxwell; Deseret Book Co.; Salt Lake City, Utah; 1987; 63-64).

Because of its competitive nature, pride creates stress and tension instead of peace and joy. Being competitive, pride is exclusive. It judges, forms cliques, and keeps people out; whereas the gospel is inclusive. It should work through His Church, with love, to bring people in.

Certainly, as we teach the gospel, we should want everyone to accept all the mercy possible. The goal of the gospel appears to be to persuade mankind, through love, to accept as much mercy as they are willing to accept as early on as possible for their own peace and joy. This is the entire effort of the Church organization.

Nevertheless we, like Javert, too often focus on justice or have serious misconceptions about mercy.

A mission president once told me of a missionary who was in the throes of anguish because he had taught his parents the gospel and they had rejected it. He believed he had condemned them to eternal suffering because they had heard and not heeded and, according to his understanding, would not have another chance. We need not fear missionary work thinking that, if our timing is off or if others aren't ready, we are condemning them to some punishment. Our Father in Heaven wants all of His children back. There is time and opportunity aplenty. Most people need multiple contacts with the gospel before accepting it.

In another instance, a teenager who had strayed was being encouraged by her Young Women's leader to return to church. Replied the young woman: "They (the members) won't let me come back." The Lord certainly wants her back, but too often we are reluctant to be so merciful. We slide too much to the side of Javert.

The father of a friend of mine lived his life as a member of the Church but was apathetic, even occasionally hostile, to it. He insisted that no one even consider doing his temple work for him after his death. However, a few months following his death, my friend began receiving strong impressions that she must proceed with his work. She ignored those feelings for a time but finally concluded there was a message in them for her. She did have his work done, after which the promptings ceased. Under the plan of mercy, the opportunities continue. Therefore, we are required to do the sealing work for everyone, no matter how they lived their mortal life or what their wishes in mortality were. Their wishes and their hearts will probably change.

We must assume that "the day of this life" (Alma 34:32) continues into the spirit world and that mercy can override almost anything up until the day of judgment. Repentance continues to work. Hearts continue to be changed. Because of Jesus and the atonement, an abundance of mercy goes into effect when a person qualifies with a change of heart. Because the plan of mercy is so far reaching, justice is really the result of mercy denied. God wants all His children back. The plan provides a way. For this reason, we must seal everyone through the power of the Priesthood, because the power is in it, through the atonement, to save everyone who will. The blessing of the sealing power increases the power of mercy.

"We cannot overemphasize the value of temple marriage, the binding ties of the sealing ordinances and the standards of personal worthiness required of them. When parents keep the covenants they have made at the altar of the temple, their children will be forever bound to them" ("Our Moral Environment;" Elder Boyd K. Packer; *Ensign*; © Intellectual Reserve, Inc.; May 1992; 66).

I have read Doctrine and Covenants, Section 76, the revelation on the three degrees of glory, in light of the power of mercy, and I have wondered, even marveled at the possibilities.

— Though we speak of inheriting thrones, kingdoms, principalities, powers and dominions in eternal life (Doc. & Cov. 132:19), we are, I think, in search of mercy rather than glory. Remembering this should help keep life in perspective and our self-righteousness at bay.

— Remembering also that, according to the law of justice, we should all belong to Satan, anything better than that horrible option is part of the plan of mercy. Every degree of glory is part of the plan of mercy and each kingdom gives more and more mercy and always more than we deserve. "This is my work and my glory to bring to pass the immortality and eternal life of man" (Moses 1:39). We focus much on eternal life, but bringing to pass resurrection and immortality is also part of His work and glory, and part of the plan of mercy.

— Those who gain the mercy of the celestial kingdom are those who have accepted the full gospel of Christ, are baptized and have received the Holy Ghost, who overcome by faith and are sealed by the Holy Spirit of Promise. And they have complied with these require-ments either in mortality or in the spirit world. Perhaps receiving this fullness of mercy is that state called in the scriptures, the rest of the Lord (Doc. & Cov. 76:51-58).

— Doctrine and Covenants Section 131 states that in the celestial kingdom there are three heavens or degrees. To obtain the highest, eternal marriage is required. We have no information on the requirements for the other two degrees. We do know that not all of us are equally faithful. I sometimes wonder how I, who have such a comfortable life and few tests of my faith, will compare to the Abrahams, the Peters, the Esthers. But then I remember mercy, that God does not compare us to each other. Rather, because of mercy, we are measured only by our own circumstances and the state of our hearts.

— Those who gain the mercy of the terrestrial kingdom are honorable persons who, either on earth or beyond the veil, have accepted Jesus but not the fullness of His gospel with all the ordinances, covenants, and requirements (Doc. & Cov. 76:71-78).

— I have thought that there might even be some scriptures that contain more options than commonly assumed. For example, Doctrine and Covenants 76:79 indicates that those who are not valiant in the testimony of Jesus receive a terrestrial inheritance. This is often defined as those who have the full gospel of Christ but are not fully committed. However, with the umbrella of mercy covering our opportunities until final judgment, not only will there be plenty of time for stray sheep to return to the fold and full commitment, but "not valiant in the testimony of Jesus" might need a different definition. "Not valiant" could mean those with a testimony of Jesus who declined to accept His full gospel.

— Those who gain the mercy of the telestial kingdom did not live honorable lives. They focused their energies on willfully destroying, injuring, or taking advantage of others; and, even in the spirit world, they did not accept Jesus (although in eternity every knee shall bow and all will confess that Jesus is the Christ). They will wait in unpleasant and uncomfortable circumstances until the final phases of the resurrection (Doc.& Cov. 76:81-82, 101-106, 110).

— All those who inherit a kingdom of glory are saved from the grasp of Satan. Only a few will be ineligible for a kingdom of glory— those who lived on earth and have known the truth but have, like Satan himself, gone to great lengths to destroy the Father's work. Though they inherit a place with the devil and his angels, these Sons of Perdition will receive the mercy of the resurrection (Doc. & Cov. 76:31-39; 1 Cor. 15:22).

As we accept more and more mercy—demonstrate a loving kindness towards self and others, and quickly incorporate Christ's mercy in our lives—the harshness of the law of justice becomes more and more tempered. Caught up in competition, people are often judgmental, but the gospel way is merciful. Although excommunication is often perceived as harsh punishment (and members often respond to such with the justice mentality of Javert), it is in fact part of the plan of mercy— much like someone doing poorly in a class, being required to withdraw and then, through their own desires and works, being given the opportunity, the mercy, to start over again.

In Mosiah, chapter four, of the Book of Mormon, king Benjamin's people expressed their feelings about mercy after hearing their king's discourse on the atonement:

"...they had viewed themselves in their own carnal state, even less than the dust of the earth. And they all cried aloud with one voice, saying: O have mercy, and apply the atoning blood of Christ that we may receive forgiveness of our sins, and our hearts may be purified; for we believe in Jesus Christ, the Son of God, who created heaven and earth, and all things; who shall come down among the children of men.

"And it came to pass that after they had spoken these words the Spirit of the Lord came upon them, and they were filled with joy, having received a remission of their sins, and having peace of conscience, because of the exceeding faith which they had in Jesus Christ who should come, according to the words which king Benjamin had spoken unto them" (Mosiah 4:2-3).

They were humbled and awed by the great plan of mercy. Seeing and hearing their response, king Benjamin continued to teach about mercy. He told them to continue to repent, and he taught them to give mercy to others. Kindly he suggested: "Are we not all beggars? Do we not all depend upon the same Being, even God, for all the substance which we have...?" (Mosiah 4:19).

Recognizing our common needs should develop in us a desire to give and to help.

Nevertheless, king Benjamin also cautioned that we should be merciful to ourselves: "See that all these things are done in wisdom and order, for it is not requisite that a man should run faster than he has strength" (Mosiah 4:27).

By following the counsel of king Benjamin, we would learn to give and receive mercy.

We need to understand and apply this for ourselves and for others, not only in an eternal sense, but on a daily basis. I recently recognized some simple ways in which our frame of mind continually influences the workings of mercy in our lives.

I was writing a paper in which several paragraphs were emphasized, given more importance, by printing the words in **boldface** type. As I proofread my work, I remembered the comments of a friend regarding life's challenges. He said: "When we have a little bad luck, we tend to base our lives on only a few paragraphs of our experience." As we struggle with the ups and downs in daily living and, in the process, look back over the story of our lives, too often we "**boldface**" the wrong paragraphs.

Life is a long story made up of short paragraphs of individual experiences. Each paragraph has "weight" or importance based on our perceptions of its impact on our lives. Some paragraphs are joyful, others are sorrowful. Some speak of success, others of failures. Some tell of welcome and hello, others of farewell and goodbye. Some describe the right things we've done, others describe the wrongs. By choosing how much importance to give each paragraph, we choose justice or mercy. We choose what to print in **boldface** type.

Those choices are critical. They can improve or worsen our lives. If we emphasize the wrong paragraphs and base our abilities or our value on a few negative experiences, we will constantly struggle with guilt and low self-esteem. We will question our potential and limit our self-confidence. On the other hand, there are always valuable lessons learned in every situation. If we can learn from the bad luck, wrong choices, sorrows, and failure but never print the negatives themselves in **boldface** to constantly emphasize our less than hoped for past, we will be able to accept whatever happened, find the positive elements, and move on with faith and hope.

The businessman who was unsuccessful in his last enterprise but is willing to try again because he learned and will profit from his mistakes will put the lessons and the vision, rather than the previous failure, in permanent **boldface.**

The athlete who fails to reach her objective but never gives up will print her planned achievement method, rather than the last failed attempt, in **boldface.**

The sinner who repents will, with gratitude for the atonement, **boldface** the commitment for the future not the weakness of the past.

The friend who feels betrayed, the employee who is discharged, the writer who is rejected, must all bounce back by printing positive paragraphs from their history in **boldface.**

Once we look past the crisis of the moment and see the bigger picture, we must then **boldface** positive paragraphs, realizing that even negative experiences have positive elements when we make the effort to emphasize them.

Life is a learning experience full of options and choices. It is up to us to decide which paragraphs from life we will print in **boldface**, which paragraphs we will allow to affect our choices, our attitudes, our feelings, today.

Overlaying life with mercy smooths out the rough spots and permits the cultivation of humility and of faith, hope, and charity. The policeman, Javert, was a confused and unhappy man because he did not understand mortality's realities. He was destroyed by his attitude of absolute justice.

Understanding the extensive availability of mercy in our Father's plan was, to me, like the frosting on the cake, the exclamation mark in *Hallelujah!* Through understanding mercy, any quicksand remaining in my life simply evaporated. Though there is a law of justice and some requirements and responsibilities therein related, that law is controlled and tamed by the plan of mercy, the great plan of happiness. It is truly a plan worth shouting about.

Psalm 136:

O give thanks unto the Lord; for he is good: for his mercy endureth for ever.

O give thanks unto the God of gods: for his mercy endureth for ever.

O give thanks to the Lord of lords: for his mercy endureth for ever.

To him who alone doeth great wonders: for his mercy endureth for ever.

To him that by wisdom made the heavens: for his mercy endureth for ever.

To him that stretched out the earth above the waters: for his mercy endureth for ever.

To him that made great lights: for his mercy endureth for ever:

The sun to rule by day: for his mercy endureth for ever:

The moon and stars to rule by night: for his mercy endureth for ever...

Who remembered us in our low estate: for his mercy endureth for ever.

And hath redeemed us from our enemies: for his mercy endureth for ever.

Who giveth food to all flesh: for his mercy endureth for ever.

O give thanks unto the God of heaven: for his mercy endureth for ever.

HAPPY THOUGHTS!

One of mortality's realities is that our learning never stops. I know I still have much to learn about the gospel.

The principles in this book are principles that have given me an infinite amount of peace and joy. Because it took many years for me to learn them and incorporate them in my life, I know that without them life can be very stressful.

We have juxtaposed social expectations against the gospel so consistently that we often cannot tell one from the other. We must accept that they are two different lifestyles—and they are incompatible. The social quicksand yields conformity, rigidity, insensitivity, and fear whereas the gospel provides individuality, flexibility, love, and confidence. Only when we separate the true gospel principles from the competitive world view can we understand the truth: sweet is the peace the gospel brings. We can lay our burden, even the stress of unrealistic social expectations and perfectionism, at His feet and be healed.

My years of unhappiness were caused by something I choose to name an "attitude disorder." It was a result of replacing the realities of mortality and our Father's plan that was set up to compensate for them with unrealistic expectations. I know that many other people have a similar problem, similar misunderstandings. However, another segment of the population suffers from unhappiness because of physiology. It is also a reality of mortality that our complex biological system does not always work perfectly. If we are unable to find happiness, it is important for us to seek answers on all reasonable routes remembering that "men (and women) are that they might have joy."

Whether we find the truth through personal study, the help of friends and loved ones, professional medical assistance or counseling, or even pure inspiration, some of the principles we need to learn and apply are:

— Accepting mortality's realities, the consequences of the fall and the blessings of the atonement, and shaking off the shackles of perfectionism.

194

— Understanding the impact of social expectations, and rejecting those that conflict with truth.

— Taming the pretense and masquerade, thereby finding the peace of being ourselves.

— Learning to live by the flexibility of the spirit of the law instead of the structure of the letter.

— Accepting our divine worth and, with the help of the Spirit, acquiring the mind power to generate faith and hope.

— Developing charity that never faileth, accompanied by humility and mercy.

Once we begin to live by these gospel principles, we will know why we once shouted for joy: ***There really is a Great Plan of Happiness!***